THE INTROVERT'S GUIDE TO SUCCESSFUL BUSINESS CONVERSATIONS

A PRACTICAL APPROACH TO OVERCOME PERFORMANCE ANXIETY, STRENGTHEN YOUR SOCIAL SKILLS, AND ADVANCE YOUR CAREER WHILE BEING YOUR AUTHENTIC SELF

AVERY HARPER

© **Copyright 2025 - All rights reserved.**

The content contained within this book may not be reproduced, duplicated, or transmitted without direct written permission from the author or the publisher.

Under no circumstances will any blame or legal responsibility be held against the publisher, or author, for any damages, reparation, or monetary loss due to the information contained within this book, either directly or indirectly.

Legal Notice:

This book is copyright protected. It is only for personal use. You cannot amend, distribute, sell, use, quote, or paraphrase any part, or the content within this book, without the author or publisher's permission.

Disclaimer Notice:

Please note that the information contained within this document is for educational and entertainment purposes only. All effort has been executed to present accurate, up-to-date, reliable, complete information. No warranties of any kind are declared or implied. Readers acknowledge that the author is not rendering legal, financial, medical, or professional advice. The content within this book has been derived from various sources. Please consult a licensed professional before attempting any techniques outlined in this book.

By reading this document, the reader agrees that under no circumstances is the author responsible for any losses, direct or indirect, that are incurred due to the use of the information in this document, including, but not limited to, errors, omissions, or inaccuracies.

ISBN Kindle:979-8-9906002-6-3

ISBN Paperback: 979-8-9906002-7-0

CONTENTS

Introduction   7

1. UNDERSTANDING THE INTROVERT ADVANTAGE   11
   The Science Behind Introversion and Communication   12
   The Gift of Active Listening   14
   Empathy as a Communication Superpower   20
   The Power of Thoughtful Reflection in Dialogue   26

2. BUILDING CONFIDENCE FOR BUSINESS INTERACTIONS   31
   Turning Anxiety Into Positive Energy: Identify and Reframe   35
   The Art of Self-Validation and Positive Reinforcement   41
   Speaking Up Without Fear: Handling Meetings and Presentations   44
   Techniques for Effective Participation   47

3. ENHANCING VERBAL COMMUNICATION SKILLS   51
   Speech Mechanics   54
   Structuring Your Thoughts for Clear and Concise Expression   56
   The Introvert's Guide to Persuasion   61

4. EMBRACING NONVERBAL
   COMMUNICATION   69
   Using Facial Expressions to Enhance Your
   Message   73
   The Impact of Gestures and Posture on
   Communication   77
   Aligning Verbal and Nonverbal
   Communication for Consistency   82

5. ENERGIZING TECHNIQUES FOR
   INTROVERTS   87
   Strategies for Recharging Quickly   90
   Maintaining Focus During Prolonged
   Meetings   94
   Setting Boundaries to Protect Your
   Energy   99
   Creating a Personal Work Recharge Plan   105

6. ENHANCING DAILY WORKPLACE
   RELATIONSHIPS   109
   Small Talk and Beyond   113
   Improving Work Conversations   116

7. HANDLING ON-THE-SPOT
   INTERACTIONS WITH EASE   123
   The Pause Before You Speak   124
   Reframing   125
   Breathing Exercises to Stay Calm and
   Composed   128
   Quick Thinking and Adaptability Skills   129

8. COMMUNICATING WITH AUTHORITY
   FIGURES   133
   Building Rapport With Authority Figures   136
   Strategies for Effective Upward
   Communication   138

Handling Rejection and Feedback With
Grace 142
Balancing Assertiveness and Diplomacy in
Real Time 146

9. MASTERING NEGOTIATION
DIALOGUES 151
Strategies for Preparation 154
Techniques for Execution 157
Identifying Win-Win Outcomes 162

10. STRATEGIES FOR CONFIDENT
NETWORKING 167
Elevator Pitches 171
Follow Up After Networking Events 177

11. CONTINUING TO BUILD YOUR
COMMUNICATIONS REPERTOIRE 185
Communicating Across Cultures 188

12. MORE INTERACTIVE EXERCISES AND
SELF-ASSESSMENT 197
Sustaining Long-Term Communication
Growth 200

Conclusion 207
References 211

INTRODUCTION

I came, I saw, I left early.

Whew, that was close. I almost had to socialize.

— UNKNOWN

If the phrases above describe you, let me tell you about Brené Brown. You might recognize her name from reading one of her six #1 *New York Times* bestsellers or listening to her podcasts, *Unlocking Us* and *Dare to Lead*. She's given multiple TED talks, and even Oprah interviewed her (brenebrown.com). But, speaking of her childhood, she said, "I felt different as an introvert in a family where introversion was mistaken for weakness and extroversion for confidence" (Brown, 2021).

This introvert turned storyteller and professor engages deeply with her audiences, connecting with them emotionally. She builds rapport through authenticity and genuine interaction. People see her as the real thing. In *The Gifts of Imperfection,* she wrote: "Authenticity is a collection of choices that we have to make every day. It's about the choice to show up and be real. The choice to be honest. The choice to let our true selves be seen" (Brené Brown, 2010). You could call Brown a successful business communicator who has stayed true to her introverted self.

This is what *The Introvert's Guide to Successful Business Conversations* is all about. The goal is to empower you, the introverted professional, to navigate business conversations effectively while staying true to who you are. By shifting the narrative, you will see your introverted traits not as limitations but as superpowers. Introverts like you often possess qualities like thoughtfulness, creativity, and the ability to connect deeply with others. These are invaluable in any business setting. Your ability to listen and think before you speak can be a tremendous asset.

This book begins with understanding the science behind introversion and your innate communication preferences. In the pages that follow, you will gain insights into overcoming your fear of speaking up as you build robust communication strategies. You'll learn to master both verbal and nonverbal communication. We will guide you through specific business scenarios, providing examples and action steps. We'll cover impromptu interactions, daily conversations, group meetings, negotiations, meetings with superiors, and networking events.

This is your first step toward transforming your business conversations. You have the ability to succeed while remaining true to yourself. When you embrace your introverted strengths and use them to communicate effectively in business, you can achieve great things. Now it's time to move from "Whew, that was close" to being a confident communicator who knows the following:

Confident introverts don't avoid social situations. They just make wise choices.

— UNKNOWN

1

UNDERSTANDING THE INTROVERT ADVANTAGE

In *Forbes*, Lien de Paul called introverted entrepreneurs "reflection ninjas," "masters of deep work," "listening legends," and "creative problem solvers" (de Paul, 2024). This is absolutely true. We introverts are known for being deep thinkers, great listeners, and empathetic. We favor meaningful dialogue over small talk. Yet, no two introverts are exactly alike. Each of us brings a different combination of introverted superpowers to the table: active listening, empathy, and reflective thinking. This chapter will explore how to harness your natural tendencies to thrive in business environments. We'll delve into the science that makes introverts unique and how you can leverage these traits for success.

This chapter isn't just about understanding introversion. It's about celebrating it. Whether you're crunching numbers or telling stories, your introverted qualities are assets.

THE SCIENCE BEHIND INTROVERSION AND COMMUNICATION

Introversion has its roots in the brain's structure and chemistry, so let's dive into the fascinating world of brain science. Your introverted brain is buzzing with activity, especially in the frontal lobes, which are responsible for analysis and rational thought. A University of Iowa study reveals that introverts have more neural activity in the frontal lobes and anterior thalamus, the areas associated with deep thinking and planning (*The Neuroscience Behind Introversion*, n.d.). Introverts carry thicker gray matter, which means we process and release information differently from our extroverted counterparts. This biological makeup allows introverts to focus longer and delve deeper into subjects, giving us distinct advantages in thoughtful communication and problem-solving. A staggering 70% of gifted individuals tend toward introversion (*Cerebral Blood Flow and Personality*, 1999).

As introverts, we also have higher baseline cortical arousal levels, which means we are more sensitive to external stimuli. This sensitivity can lead to overstimulation in environments that extroverts might find energizing. We process the neurotransmitter dopamine linked to pleasure and reward differently, too. While extroverts thrive on the dopamine rush from social interactions, introverts can find it overwhelming. We prefer environments where we can dive deep into thought rather than skimming the surface. This biological foundation makes us favor depth over breadth when we communicate (*The Neuroscience Behind Introversion*, n.d.).

To put it more scientifically, extroverts are linked with dopamine/adrenaline, energy-spending, and sympathetic nervous systems. This sympathetic nervous system activates the fight or flight response. However, the introvert's nervous system is connected more with the neurotransmitter acetylcholine. Our introverted nervous systems conserve energy and are parasympathetic. This parasympathetic nervous system restores the body to a state of calm. As introverts, we require a limited range of dopamine (not too little or too much) and good levels of acetylcholine to feel calm and without depression or anxiety (Kane, 2023).

Extroverts might jump into a conversation while their thoughts are still forming. But your introverted brain prefers to mull things over. It's a reflection of your brain's penchant for reflective processing. Your brain needs a moment before responding, which some interpret as hesitation. But this pause is a strategic advantage that allows you to consider all angles of a problem and deliver solutions that are well thought out and innovative. You naturally excel in situations requiring thoughtful reflection and analysis. This depth of thinking is particularly valuable in business conversations, where quick, superficial responses often miss the mark.

THE GIFT OF ACTIVE LISTENING

In a quiet conference room, the kind where every creak of a chair or shuffle of paper seems amplified, active listening is a formidable asset. When it's noisy, it's the quiet individual who often captures the most insights. More than just a soft skill, active listening is often hailed as an introvert's superpower, especially in business settings that frequently champion speaking. This strategic advantage enables introverts to navigate complex interpersonal landscapes. To listen actively, you must shift focus from your internal conversation to the other person's communication. You display self-control by shutting down your internal dialogue and avoiding daydreaming. When you listen actively, you give speakers your full attention, engaging with their words and responding thoughtfully. You are genuinely interested. It's the difference between hearing and truly listening.

An active listener is not a passive presence. You become involved using nonverbal affirmations like nodding and maintaining eye contact, signaling that you are with the speaker every step of the way. Active listening also involves absorbing the nuances of tone, the pauses that carry weight, and the unspoken cues that reveal more than mere dialogue.

Critical listening is *not* active listening. The goal of active listening is for others to feel heard and supported. It requires patience and doesn't try to fill periods of silence with your own thoughts or stories. It gives people time to think without finishing their sentences for them. It makes the conversation more about that other person than yourself (Cuncic, 2024).

Active listening is your tool for gathering insights that might otherwise go unnoticed. You can identify unspoken needs and underlying motivations, providing a deeper understanding of the situation. You pay attention to what's not being said. These insights can inform decisions that align with your company's goals and values, fostering a sense of unity and purpose. For example, during a team meeting, introvert Charles noticed a colleague's hesitance when discussing a new project. By addressing this concern privately, he gained insights into potential roadblocks and worked to facilitate a solution that benefits the entire team.

Listening also plays a pivotal role in conflict resolution. In tense moments, the ability to listen attentively can defuse high emotions and redirect the conversation toward constructive dialogue where both parties feel understood. By acknowledging others' perspectives and showing empathy, you can mitigate disagreements. Imagine a scenario where two departments are at odds over resource allocation. Introverted leader Amanda might facilitate a dialogue that allows each side to voice their frustrations while she listens for commonalities. By identifying shared goals, Amanda can guide the group toward a resolution that satisfies all involved.

Sadly, much to our partner's and coworkers' disappointment, not every introvert is an excellent listener. However, you can cultivate and hone active listening skills using the techniques mentioned below. Let's start with what you must stop doing.

Stop judging. The person on the other end of your conversation should not be shamed, criticized, blamed, or otherwise negatively received. Admittedly, we each have biases and prejudices. But these block us from listening effectively. You must put aside your preconceived notions about the speaker. Perhaps you've already formed an opinion about his or her ideas, which can cloud your ability to listen impartially. Acknowledge your bias, and then move past it. Otherwise, you might tune out an important insight or novel idea that person presents. Make it your goal to withhold judgment. This includes not giving advice (Cuncic, 2024).

Don't interrupt. It may be stating the obvious, but it needs to be said. It's tempting to jump in with your thoughts. But everyone hates to be cut off mid-sentence. It's derailing, distracting, and disrespectful. Wait until you're sure the other person has finished speaking. Otherwise, you limit your understanding of the speaker's message. Remember: Patience is a virtue, and silence is golden (Burton, 2023).

Now, let's move on to positive actions to develop your active listening skills.

Eliminate distractions, especially the biggest one, your phone. In today's open-office settings or during virtual meetings, a ringing phone or a notification ping can easily divert your attention. Maybe the answer is as simple as silencing your phone or choosing a quiet spot for important conversations. Stop multitasking and looking at your devices. Addressing these barriers proactively makes you more present and attentive.

People can tell when someone isn't paying attention to them. Don't be that person.

Show you are engaged in the discussion. Make eye contact, lean forward slightly, and nod. Use verbal cues to acknowledge what the other person is saying, like "Uh huh" or "I see." You want to show that you are following closely. This encourages your counterpart to continue speaking.

Specifically, excessive eye contact can be weird or creepy and make the other person uncomfortable. You can use the 50/70 rule to keep this from happening. Maintain eye contact for 50 to 70% of your listening time. Hold your contact for 4 to 5 seconds before you briefly look away (Schultz, 2012).

Listen for more than just words. Nonverbal cues tell a story, too. Pay attention to the other person's body language, including their facial expressions, posture, tone of voice, and behavior. If your counterpart is talking fast, for instance, he might be nervous or anxious. If said person is talking slowly, she might be tired or just an introvert like you, carefully choosing her words (Cuncic, 2024).

Ask open-ended questions. Yes/no questions dead-end because they don't encourage further responses. Open-ended questions reassure your coworkers or clients that you're interested in what they have to say. You value their input and are genuinely interested. You gain the most information from these types of questions (Burton, 2023). Good starter questions include: Can you tell me a bit more about that? What do you think about that? What do you suggest we do? (Cuncic, 2024).

Be a sounding board. Reflect back what you hear using paraphrasing or summarizing. This minimizes miscommunication. "In other words, what you are saying…" and "I'm hearing that…" give the other person an opportunity to say whether you've captured their message. If not, ask for clarification. But think of the big picture rather than focusing on the smaller details (Cuncic, 2024).

Learn from others. Watch skilled interviewers on TV or listen to them on talk radio. Or do online research on active listening. Verywell Mind has a podcast focused on active listening advice: "#91 Why It Benefits You to Become a Better Listener" (Morin, 2020).

Action Plan

- **Recognizing your bias:** Choose two coworkers with whom you find it frustrating to communicate. Write out any preconceived notions you have about these individuals. How

have you stereotyped them? What do you know about their situations and/or motivations? Challenge your bias by finding out one nonwork-related interesting fact about each person.
- **Distractions:** Name 1–3 distractions keeping you from actively listening at work. Remove one of these distractions (i.e., turn off notifications or block visual access to something that always catches your eye).

EMPATHY AS A COMMUNICATION SUPERPOWER

Empathy is about emotional connection. It allows us to step into others' shoes, seeing the world from their perspective. Empathy recognizes our emotions and those of others, using this awareness to manage interactions thoughtfully. Most introverts possess a keen sense of introspection, making them naturally empathetic. If that's you, your empathy superpower naturally flows into your communications. Hurray! If not, fear not. Your empathy skills can be honed.

But first, we must distinguish the difference between sympathy and empathy as they're often confused. Sympathy feels pity for another person without really understanding what it's like to be in their circumstances. Empathy is the capacity to imagine oneself in the other person's situation, including experiencing that person's emotions, opinions, and ideas. This is why we send sympathy cards when someone dies. Even those without an emotional connection to the deceased's family can perform this gesture. But it's the empathic person who "gets it." It's the difference between the people who visit the funeral home to pay their respects vs. those who genuinely care (*Using Empathy in Communication, n.d.*).

Certain communication behaviors kill empathy. Many of these you'll recognize easily because you find them annoying also:

- criticizing
- challenging the legitimacy of the speaker's feelings
- giving advice
- interrupting
- changing the subject

When we allow these barriers to creep into our conversations, our coworkers will close down. After all, who appreciates unsolicited advice? No one. Work hard to eliminate these bad habits from your speech, both personally and professionally.

Judgmental attitudes kill empathetic/empathic communication as well. It's worth mentioning again what was stated above: We must acknowledge our biases and stereotypes. This enables us to pause, extend grace, and listen without judgment. Practically speaking, "you" statements sound accusatory. Replace them with "I" statements to convey concern without judgment. "Why" questions can be taken as confrontational. Replace them with "how," "who," "when," and "where" questions. Better yet, questions like "What do you need right now?" or "How can I support you?" show empathy for others. But they must be accompanied by compassionate listening. If you aren't there, don't be disingenuous (Sen, 2024).

We know how to bar empathy, so let's switch to cultivating it. Empathetic communication focuses on goodwill and doing no harm, prioritizing people and their well-being (Team Duarte, 2024). Per the Grossman Group, you can achieve empathetic communication using these six steps (*Using Empathy in Communication, n.d.*):

1. Listen without interruption.
2. Pause and imagine how the other person feels (How would you like to be treated if the roles were reversed?).

3. Let your listeners know you hear them by reflecting on what they have said: "What I hear you saying is…"
4. Validate feelings: "I understand that you are feeling…"
5. Offer support and then close the conversation.
6. Follow up on how they are going once an appropriate amount of time has passed.

Put another way, you achieve empathetic communication by listening actively, acknowledging the other party's emotions, and responding with care. It's about being present. You are communicating with the intention to hear and support others, with the goal that they feel heard and understood (Sen, 2024).

Here are some examples of empathy-driven communication you can use to build rapport and foster genuine relationships. Imagine your team members are anxious about an upcoming project. As the team leader, you don't dismiss their feelings. Instead, you take the time to ask each team member what is causing them to stress about the project. You will not only alleviate immediate concerns but also strengthen the team's cohesion and create a supportive work environment.

If you have to share hard news, like downsizing, use a compassionate tone rather than a "business as usual" demeanor. Work to make eye contact. Don't talk about how the bad news impacts you. The timing isn't right. Put yourself in their shoes when crafting your message (Team Duarte, 2024).

During conflict resolution, allow parties to express their perspectives without fear of judgment, fostering a space where consensus can emerge. Imagine you are an introverted manager facing a team member angry about a perceived slight. Instead of responding defensively, you take a moment to listen and acknowledge the team member's feelings. This act of empathetic listening defuses tension and opens the door to constructive dialogue. In mediation, when an aggressive client challenges your proposal, you can respond empathetically by validating their concerns while gently guiding the conversation toward a resolution.

When one party feels sidelined at a negotiation table, you pick up on this subtle discomfort and address it directly. For example, you might invite the quieter party to give more input or rephrase points to ensure clarity. This not only smooths the negotiation process but also builds trust between parties.

Kindness and good relationships foster empathy, so the exercises below include two activities to put your coworkers first. Goodwill is contagious.

Action Plan: Honing Empathy

- Write down what makes three of your coworkers passionate, happy, or sad. If you don't know, please ask. Your curiosity will endear you to them.
- Write down two things about yourself to share with coworkers. Benign examples include your favorite ice cream flavor, sports team, or movie.
- Do a random act of kindness for a coworker: buy them a cup of coffee, send an e-card, dust the snow off their windshield, or bring treats for everyone.
- Write down two more empathetic phrases. I will give you, "That must be really tough for you." Speak them out loud until they become natural for you.

THE POWER OF THOUGHTFUL REFLECTION IN DIALOGUE

> *I insist on a lot of time being spent, almost every day, to just sit and think. That is very uncommon in American business. I read and think. So I do more reading and thinking, and make less impulse decisions than most people in business. I do it because I like this kind of life.*
>
> — WARREN BUFFET (SCHWANTES, 2021)

Like introvert Warren Buffet, your thicker gray matter predisposes you to think deeply, thoroughly analyze, achieve clarity, and make well-informed, well-considered decisions.

Your quiet power of reflection allows for a deeper understanding of complex topics and enhances clarity in dialogue. Consider how many successful professionals, like Bill Gates, take time to reflect before making decisions. Gates famously retreats for "Think Weeks" to dive into books and ideas, emerging with innovative solutions. Per Cain, introverts tend to "think before they act, digest information thoroughly, stay on task longer, give up less easily, and work more accurately" (Cain, 2013).

Let's spell out the advantage of your introverted superpower more thoroughly. Your reflective thinking leads you to:

- **Deep thinking and analysis:** Introverts analyze complex problems, synthesize large amounts of information, and notice subtle patterns (Westover, 2024).
- **Focus and concentration:** Introverts can zero in on key tasks for extended periods without distraction (Laney, 2013).
- **Strategic decision-making:** Introverts are analytical and deliberate. They carefully weigh options from all angles. They're well suited for strategic planning and making complex decisions (Stevens, 2017).
- **Creative thinking:** Introverts think "outside of the box." They notice new connections and envision innovative solutions (Cain, 2013).
- **Reluctant to take risks:** Introverts are conservative, making fewer rash decisions and mistakes (Cain, 2013).

Unlike active listening and empathy, this reflective thinking superpower is either something you have or you don't. You can leverage it but not create it. Be happy you're an introvert.

The best way to leverage this strength is to create time and space to make it happen. Your boss is unlikely to give you a "Think Week." Nor do you have Buffett's authority to allow you to sit, read, and think. But you can incorporate deep thinking times into your work routines by being intentional. It starts with your workspace. Most introverts find themselves at odds with typical work environments because they're mostly tailored for extroverts. Managing distractions is problematic. But you can organize what's yours. Declutter your desk and the surrounding area to minimize mental distractions. Use noise-blocking tools. You might even add some elements that make you calm or give you inspiration, like soothing lighting or a plant (Chazin, 2024).

Try "task batching" by grouping similar tasks and tackling them together in a focused period. Constantly switching between different types of work can disrupt your focus and exhaust you mentally. Task batching allows you to stay in the same mental modes and reduces the cognitive load you get from switching tasks (Chazin, 2024).

Use your prime time for deep work. Your prime time is when you're most focused and energized. Typically, it's when you do your best work. Schedule your most mentally demanding tasks for that period. It's your deep work time for tasks requiring your full attention. You might even schedule focus blocks in your calendar for uninterrupted work time. Sadly, you may need to protect them. But we'll be covering boundaries and your energy supply more in Chapter 5 (Chazin, 2024).

Employers are starting to get the message that we introverts need our time and space to be our most productive. The New York Times covered the story of a tech company that created "hush rooms" so their many introverted coders could concentrate (Reynolds, 2019). Harvard Business Review ran an article on a global consulting firm that instituted "introvert hour" every afternoon. Meetings were banned during that time frame. The productivity and engagement of their introverts grew because they had protected reflection time (Jones, 2020). Maybe you could leverage a group of your introverted friends at work to suggest one of these measures. At the very least, you could give your supervisor the article links.

Action Plan: Thoughtful Reflection

- **Reflection hour:** Choose the time and location for an hour of personal reflection time per week. Put it on your calendar. Do the same thing with your work schedule twice a week or create at least one focus block time.
- **Task-batching:** Give task-batching a try. Choose more repetitive or less demanding tasks to group together.

2

BUILDING CONFIDENCE FOR BUSINESS INTERACTIONS

Frank Perdue was a shy child, a shy teenager, and a shy adult; his widow, Mitzi, even said, "To the end of his days, he was basically a shy man." Yet Perdue overcame his shyness and built the poultry business empire Perdue Farms, which became synonymous with quality poultry and innovative business practices. Perdue's journey from a timid salesman to a powerhouse in the poultry industry is a testament to the power of overcoming shyness (Wayshak, 2015). His story is a beacon for introverts who feel overshadowed in the bustling business world.

Not every introvert is shy. But, if you are like Perdue, understanding the roots of your shyness is the first step toward overcoming it. Often, shyness stems from a blend of past experiences, self-doubt, and fear of judgment, essentially in times when you have felt insecure. Only certain situations trigger shyness, and you can identify them. Think about when you've been socially anxious at work. What do these situations have in common? What made you feel insecure? Once you've identified your triggers, analyze which of the suggestions given below you could use to combat them.

The first is to combat your negative self-talk. Shyness whispers lies about your capabilities, convincing you that your voice doesn't matter and your input lacks value. The lies say, "I don't have anything valuable to add to this conversation." But that's simply not true. You have a unique perspective to share. Stop self-sabotaging. Replace your negative self-talk with truthful, positive self-talk like, "I know a thing or two about this subject" or "I am on the ball at work." Repeat them aloud. Create a mental affirmation loop tape in your brain to which you redirect your thoughts when the lies creep in. (More on self-affirmation is coming soon!)

Focus on your strengths. In your shy moments, you focus on what you can't do well, which creates more anxiety and perpetuates negativity. But you have many strengths. List what you already know about your project or company. Did your education or experience give you expertise about a certain subject pertaining to work? List it. (Like Perdue, you too could become an expert in your field through constant learning.) List all the project goals and achievements you've already accomplished. Perhaps you figured out the system glitch that was holding up your team. "Then read your list before going into a situation where you usually feel shy. By keeping your strengths top-of-mind, you'll be more relaxed and confident in yourself" (Winter, 2022). By embracing your strengths, you can turn your shyness into a platform for growth and potential.

Focusing on the other participants in the interaction draws you out of yourself also. Get out of your head by actively listening to what people are saying around you. Observe the group dynamics. Leverage your introvert superpowers. Ask follow-up questions: "Why did you say that?" or "Would you please tell me more?" While the other person is answering your question, you can take a moment to recompose yourself. Ask more and talk less (Winter, 2022).

Preparation can be your ally in overcoming shyness. If going to the water cooler makes you anxious, take a look at the news before work to give you ideas for conversations. Before meetings, study the agenda and outline what your potential contributions are. Don't procrastinate when it comes to presentations. If you feel rushed or ill-prepared, you'll become more anxious. Do your homework in advance, so that you will be more relaxed. Practice your presentation aloud multiple times to build confidence and lock your outline and keywords into your brain. This preparation boosts your confidence and allows you to speak with authority.

Because you aren't shy around your friends, work to make one or two friends at work. Invite them to have coffee or sit together at the cafeteria. Ask if they would like to walk with you during lunch break. If your company offers clubs, join one that piques your interest. Get to know a few of your coworkers as individuals. You will become more confident working with these people in your professional environment if they are your friends also (*Tips to Stop Shyness From Holding You Back at Work*, n.d.).

Action Plan: Overcoming Shyness

- **Identify triggers:** Document 2–4 recent times when you felt socially anxious on the job. Write down what made you insecure in each situation. (This could be a memory of interacting with the same person in the past.) Did you notice any patterns? Write down strategies to employ next time with each situation.

- **Identify strengths:** Write down 2–4 strengths you bring to your workplace.
- **Potential friends:** Identify two potential coworkers to befriend. Do an activity together such as getting coffee or sitting together at lunch.

TURNING ANXIETY INTO POSITIVE ENERGY: IDENTIFY AND REFRAME

You're sitting at the end of a long conference table moments before an important presentation. Your heart is racing, and your palms are sweaty. That familiar knot tightens in your stomach. The meeting hasn't even started. But your mind is already spiraling with thoughts of what could go wrong. The anticipation of difficult questions looms large, casting a shadow over your ability to think clearly. You envision scenarios where you're caught off guard, struggling to find the right words. This anxiety can feel paralyzing, making the very idea of participating seem daunting. This is a familiar scene for many introverts.

Put a name to what is triggering your meeting anxiety. Sometimes, it's the anticipation of the unknown that fuels anxiety. You might worry about being put on the spot and asked questions you're unprepared to answer. This fear can lead to over-preparation, which can heighten your stress level rather than mitigate it. If you're prone to over-preparation, set a limit on the amount of preparation time you allow yourself. Also, shift to focusing on the strengths you bring to the table. You're a careful listener, capable of synthesizing information and offering thoughtful insights. These qualities are valuable, even if they manifest differently from more extroverted colleagues. (Please note that Chapter 7 focuses more on impromptu interactions and includes breathing exercises.)

The fear of speaking in front of peers is another common trigger. It's not just about finding the courage to speak up; it's the worry of how your words will be perceived. Will you sound knowledgeable? Will your ideas be dismissed or, worse, criticized? This fear of judgment can lead to self-doubt, overshadowing your confidence. The pressure to contribute on the spot adds another layer of complexity. In fast-paced meetings, where decisions are made in real time, introverts might struggle to articulate thoughts as quickly as their extroverted counterparts. This demand for instant responses can be overwhelming, pushing you further into the background.

Your emotions are connected to the thoughts or events that triggered them, so tracking them is important. Think back to the last two business meetings you attended. What emotions did you experience before, during, and after the meetings? Perhaps you felt a sense of dread leading up to the meeting yet experienced relief once it concluded. What were you dreading pre-meeting? Why did you feel relieved post-meeting? What emotions were sandwiched in the middle during the meeting? Were you called upon to speak? If so, how did you respond emotionally? Or maybe there was a moment when you managed to share your thoughts, and the positive reception boosted your confidence. Both your negative and positive emotions merit being noted. The negative ones point out your anxiety triggers, while the positive feelings build your resilience as a communicator.

Once you have identified your anxiety triggers, you can use reframing to shift your perspective from negativity to positivity. Formally, this technique is called cognitive reframing or cognitive restructuring. You reframe your thoughts about meetings by seeing them as opportunities for shared growth and learning rather than as a performance (*How to Cope With Social Anxiety*, 2019). You relabel your anxiety as caring about your work and coworkers, which allows you to channel the energy into your participation. This mindset can ease the pressure to be perfect, allowing you to participate more freely. Remind yourself that everyone in the room is there to contribute, not to critique each other harshly. Meetings are a platform for exchanging ideas and fostering collaboration. You bring your work experiences and strengths or expertise to the table so you can begin to approach meetings with a sense of confidence and purpose (*Reframing Negative Thoughts*, n.d.).

Reframing your past experiences aids you in reframing future events. Think back to a time when anxiety loomed large over a work task or meeting. How could you reinterpret that situation through the lens of excitement? Perhaps the tension you felt was not a signal of impending failure but a cue for heightened focus and creativity. For example, if an impending deadline induces anxiety, view it as a challenge to showcase your organizational skills and ability to deliver under pressure. By rewriting the narrative, you can begin to see anxious energy not as a foe to be vanquished but as an ally in your professional arsenal.

A second type of reframing finds its basis in physiology. Your anxiety causes a rush of sensations not unlike the feeling of excitement. In fact, your body's responses are strikingly similar: It prepares for action, whether it's a daunting task or an exhilarating opportunity. This overlap between anxiety and excitement forms the basis of an intriguing psychological connection. By reframing anxiety as excitement, you can transform anxiety into a source of energy and motivation. For example, if you feel nervous before a big job interview, you can actively reframe those nerves as "excited anticipation" for the opportunity to showcase your skills or start a new adventure. This essentially transforms your anxious feelings into a more positive energy (Brooks, 2013).

Consider seasoned public speaker Chad's experience as another example of consciously transforming anxiety into positivity. Before stepping onto the stage, he feels the familiar twinge of nerves. Instead of succumbing to anxiety, Chad embraces the rush as a sign of readiness, using it to fuel an engaging and lively presentation. This transformation isn't limited to the stage. Business professionals often leverage this reframing technique to enhance their performance in everyday scenarios. Take marketing executive Susan, for instance. Preparing to pitch a new campaign, she's initially overwhelmed by the stakes. However, she chooses to channel her anxiety into creativity, allowing it to drive innovative ideas that captivate her audience.

Reflecting on your own experiences can be a powerful tool for reframing. Think back to a time when anxiety loomed large over a work task or meeting. How could you reinterpret that situation through the lens of excitement? Perhaps the tension you felt was not a signal of impending failure but a cue for heightened focus and creativity. For example, if a looming deadline induces anxiety, view it as a challenge to showcase your organizational skills and ability to deliver under pressure. By rewriting the narrative, you can begin to change your anxious energy into an ally in your professional arsenal.

Sometimes, it helps to verbalize your shift from anxiety to excitement. You might repeat phrases like, "I'm excited for this challenge" or "This is going to be great." Speaking something aloud helps you to internalize it. Your anticipation opens the door to increased motivation and engagement. When you approach a situation with excitement, you're more likely to participate actively, offering insights and ideas that might remain hidden under a veil of anxiety. Reciting phrases like those above enhances your confidence and presence, allowing you to stand out in professional settings.

Action Plan

- **Recording anxious moments:** Write down the moments you were anxious at work last week. During the next month, continue writing down your anxious moments. What scenarios triggered these feelings? Is there a pattern?
- **Victories:** Write down your victories as

signaled by your positive emotions. Remember that small wins add up to big victories.
- **Reframing:** Re-script two or three of the anxious moments you experience this week by identifying their potential. What good things can come from the opportunity placed before you?
- Practice saying, "I'm excited for this opportunity," "This will go well," "I've got this," or a similar sentiment in relation to the events mentioned above.

THE ART OF SELF-VALIDATION AND POSITIVE REINFORCEMENT

Imagine starting your day with a conscious acknowledgment of your own worth. Self-validation is not just a feel-good exercise; it's a powerful tool for building confidence. Mantras can serve as daily reminders of your capabilities, encouraging you to embrace your unique qualities. Many introverts like J.K. Rowling, author of the Harry Potter series, have used self-affirmations to bolster their spirits and remind themselves of their strengths. Rowling would often remind herself, "I am not afraid of storms, for I am learning how to sail my ship." (*30 of Literature's Most Inspirational Quotes about Strength,* 2019) Spanx CEO Sara Blakely's mantra is "Run with it. Ignore what everyone else says." Considering the billionaire status of both women, their mantras clearly worked for them.

In *Forbes*, Paula Marolewski illustrates the power of her mantra for networking events. She calls herself a hermit who takes "introvert" to the next level. But no one at a networking event would guess that. There she shines, even sparkles. "I boldly walk up to people I have never met. People have actually told me that they envy my ability to mix and mingle and engage people in conversation!" She does it by repeating her mantra over and over again inside her head: "Walk in and act like you own the place!" (Marolewski, n.d.).

Incorporating positive reinforcement into your daily routine can further enhance your motivation and self-esteem. This is like a feedback loop where positive behavior is encouraged and rewarded. For instance, if you successfully navigate a difficult conversation at work, reward yourself with something meaningful like a favorite snack, a leisurely walk, or a new book. Doing this creates a system where achievements, regardless of size, are celebrated. Identify what rewards resonate with you. Is it a quiet evening with a good book, or perhaps a day off to explore a new hobby? What motivates you? Use these things to tailor your rewards to keep yourself engaged and enthusiastic.

Our thoughts shape our reality, so we need to nurture an encouraging mindset. Negative self-talk undermines confidence and performance. Challenge these negative thoughts by questioning their validity. Are they grounded in reality, or are they echoes of doubt and insecurity? Replace them with positive mantras that affirm your strengths and potential. For instance, if you catch yourself thinking, *I can't do this*, reframe it into, *I am capable and prepared*. This shift in language profoundly impacts your outlook.

Action Plan

- **Rewards:** List three rewards you can give yourself as positive reinforcement.
- **Journaling:** Track your negative thoughts over the past week. Look for the patterns and triggers that contributed to this negativity.
- **Reframing:** Recast two negative thoughts into positive ones.
- **Your mantras:** Choose or craft a set of positive affirmations or mantras to encourage you. Practice them regularly, integrating them into your morning routine or before challenging tasks. Consider choosing different mantras for different settings. (It's okay to include "Fake it till you make it.")

Special note: Marolewski says not to be timid in creating your own mantras. Outrageous is good. "Be flippant. Be bold. Come up with something wacky. Doing so will make you laugh... your sense of humor will relax you even more" (Marolewski, n.d.).

SPEAKING UP WITHOUT FEAR: HANDLING MEETINGS AND PRESENTATIONS

> *Every time I went on stage I was so terrified I almost threw up. I learned why they call it the greenroom.*
>
> — SARA BLAKELY, FOUNDER AND CEO OF SPANX (O'CONNOR, 2012)

For introverts, the psychological barriers to doing presentations or speaking up in business settings can feel like an invisible fence, keeping your thoughts and ideas locked away. A common fear is the dread of being wrong. It whispers that a mistake could expose you, leading to embarrassment or loss of credibility. Yet, this fear often magnifies the consequences out of proportion. Accepting that everyone, even experts, can err is a freeing realization. Mistakes are not the end of the world. They are opportunities to learn and grow. By reframing, you shift your focus from the fear of making mistakes to the potential for contributing valuable insights. You can begin dismantling this barrier.

Hierarchy within your company can be intimidating. If you're new to your job or a junior employee, you probably feel reserved around your new coworkers or senior colleagues. You may be reluctant to share your ideas because you don't think you are in a position to do so: "I don't have enough experience yet." But don't underestimate the valuable perspective you bring. That's why you were hired in the first place. By positioning yourself as a learner, you can contribute without coming off as arrogant. Everyone's input is needed. Listen to what Reed Hastings, CEO of Netflix, said: "We now say that it is disloyal to Netflix when you disagree with an idea and do not express disagreement. By withholding your opinion, you are implicitly choosing not to help the company" (Besieux et al., 2021).

Another concern is the worry about interrupting others. This worry can be paralyzing during fast-paced discussions. Introverts often value the flow of conversation and may hesitate to interject. Your empathetic side also doesn't want to appear rude. However, identifying opportune moments to join in is a skill that you can cultivate. Begin by paying attention to natural interjection points: a pause in the speaker's delivery, a change in tone indicating a transition point, a clear shift in topic, or a nonverbal cue like raised eyebrows or people raising their hands slightly.

Research on turn-taking in conversations shows that the current speaker is likely to resume speaking after a half-second pause, feeling that others had plenty of time to jump in (Besieux et al., 2021). Therefore, signaling your intention to contribute is key. Practice aloud interjecting politely with phrases like, "I'd like to add…" or "Can I suggest…?". This approach shows respect for the existing dialogue and smoothly integrates your comments into the discussion. If the speaker asks a direct question that invites input, it's your time to shine.

Understanding the dynamics of your typical work meetings can help you find moments to contribute. Write down or verbally record what happens during these gatherings. Pay attention to the key individuals' habits. Is there a colleague who always speaks first? Or perhaps a manager who dominates the conversation? What causes the dialogue to change direction? An agenda? What cues indicate the possibility of interjecting? (Think short pauses.) Does the speaker typically invite input? Recognizing these patterns can help you identify opportunities to contribute more effectively.

Action Plan: Meeting Dynamics

- **Self-assessment:** Reflect on a recent work situation where you didn't speak up. What were the specific fears or concerns that held you back from speaking? Was it the setting, the people involved, a feeling, or perhaps the topic itself? Write down what triggered you. Be as specific as possible.
- **Interjections:** Write out three natural interjection points you observed in the last meeting. Are these repeated patterns? If so, you've identified potential input opportunities.

TECHNIQUES FOR EFFECTIVE PARTICIPATION

Fear not; strategies exist that can help you engage confidently and effectively in work meetings. One of the most potent tools in your game plan is preparation. Before the meeting, take some time to review the agenda. Identify the key points you want to address and jot them down. This process clarifies your thoughts and boosts your confidence by giving you a few well-considered points in your pocket. Then, when the time comes, you're ready to articulate your insights clearly and succinctly. If you are the speaker, include visuals in your presentation as they draw attention away from yourself. Doing this removes some of the pressure of being in the spotlight.

Beyond the necessary legwork on a computer or notepad, your preparation should include wearing clothing that's both comfortable and professional so that you feel good. Does talking to a particular person relax you? You might call that friend or family member right before the meeting, too. Then, you can carry that relaxed feeling with you into the meeting (*How to Cope With Social Anxiety*, 2019).

You may have engaged in avoidance behaviors during past meetings. These include not looking people in the eye, covering your mouth when you speak, or not talking at all. Monitor these actions going forward. If you find yourself doing them, give yourself some grace and permission to feel anxiety. But actively work to diminish them by setting realistic goals of eliminating one behavior or reducing the number of avoidance occurrences per meeting.

When the meeting time arrives, here are some pointers for speaking up: Show that you are engaged in the conversation by nodding in agreement, taking notes, and making eye contact (not possible when you are looking at a screen continually). When you want to speak, signal it nonverbally by leaning slightly forward and making direct eye contact with the speaker. When all else fails, raise your hand. (Chapter 4 focuses on nonverbal communication more extensively.) Aim to strengthen the discussion, so focus on being relevant. If you disagree, give constructive criticism with the intent to be supportive. Offering an alternative solution would be even better. Be sure to show appreciation if someone invites you to contribute also (Besieux et al., 2021). Remember also that effective participation isn't just about speaking up. It's about knowing when to listen actively, too.

Action Plan

- **Preparing to speak:** Practice your readiness to speak nonverbals (leaning forward, slightly raising your hand) and polite interjection phases in front of a mirror: "I'd like to add…. I'd like us to consider…" or "May I suggest…?" multiple times daily for the 3-4 days before your next team meeting.
- **Strategy for your next meeting:** Review the agenda. Then, identify 2–3 key moments where your input could enhance the discussion. Script your intended contributions. Practice this script aloud multiple times, refining it until you're comfortable. You are building a strong memory muscle.

- **Goals:** Set a goal to contribute once at the next meeting. Make another contribution at the following meeting. Once you attain that goal, celebrate your achievement by treating yourself. Then, move your goal to two contributions. Keep moving your goal forward until you hit four contributions, remembering to include asking for clarification and summarizing in your comments.

3

ENHANCING VERBAL COMMUNICATION SKILLS

There are two types of speakers: those that are nervous and those that are liars.

— MARK TWAIN (ZIMMER, 2009)

Whether or not you agree with his politics, Tesla's CEO, Elon Musk, is well-known for his memorable and impactful communication style. He has a blunt and sometimes unconventional approach to communication and offers his unfiltered opinions. (Billionaires get to do that.) But he is also transparent, direct, and authentic. In his public speaking, he's mastered the strategic use of pauses and visionary language. *Forbes* quoted Musk as saying, "I'm basically like an introverted engineer, so it took a lot of practice and effort to be able to go up on stage and not just stammer…" (Castrillon, 2019).

You may not be a CEO who is obliged to do public speaking engagements. But this chapter will serve as your guide to refining how you express yourself in professional settings. It's not about changing who you are but about equipping you with the tools to share your insights confidently and articulately. Think of it as tuning your instrument to ensure your voice is heard and respected. To do this, let's set the stage with some preliminaries.

To truly benefit from the strategies discussed from here on out, you must enlist a role-playing partner. This person can be a colleague or even a friend willing to engage in hypothetical business scenarios with you. Role-playing offers the opportunity to practice responses in a controlled, supportive environment. You'll be able to navigate dialogues, test out new techniques, and discover what resonates most authentically with your style. It's akin to rehearsing for a play, where you fine-tune your performance before stepping onto the stage of real-life interactions.

A trusted coworker can also play a key role in this process. Choose someone who is encouraging, honest, and perceptive enough to offer insights into areas you might not notice yourself. Someone with an aggressive personality probably isn't the best option. This coworker acts as a mirror, reflecting back both your strengths and pointing out areas for improvement. Their feedback will be invaluable in refining your communication skills. Approach this relationship with an open mind, ready to embrace constructive criticism as a stepping stone to growth. This collaboration is not just about practice; it's about building a support system that encourages you to step out of your comfort zone.

Action Plan: Find Your Communication Allies

1. Identify a colleague or friend who communicates effectively and is supportive.
2. Invite them to participate in role-playing exercises with you.
3. Choose a trusted coworker for honest feedback on your communication style.
4. Schedule regular practice sessions and feedback meetings for a minimum of half an hour weekly.

As you engage with these exercises, remember that communication is not a solitary endeavor. It thrives on interaction and exchange. By involving others in your development process, you create a dynamic learning environment where you can experiment, refine, and ultimately enhance your verbal communication skills. Never underestimate the importance of practice. "Practice makes perfect" may sound cliché. But it is still solid advice. When talking about public speaking, former First Lady Hillary Clinton puts it this way: "... nobody starts out comfortable; you have to learn how to be comfortable - practice. I cannot overstate the importance of practicing." If Musk and Clinton needed practice, so do we (*101 Quotes to Inspire Speakers*, 2016).

SPEECH MECHANICS

The first step to expressing yourself clearly is to speak clearly. This may seem simplistic, but if your words are mumbled or mispronounced, you aren't communicating intelligibly. Your enunciation is important. Pay attention to consonants, especially those at the beginning and endings of words. Changing one consonant sound can change the meaning of a word, as in "take" vs. "fake." We also use consonant sounds to distinguish when one word ends and another begins. Your audience needs your consonants to be clear so that they can recognize word boundaries. Slurred consonants make you much harder to follow.

Practicing tongue twisters improves your diction. Repeatedly saying challenging phrases trains your tongue and lips to articulate more precisely. Children compete to say tongue twisters as quickly as possible. But you need to focus on pronouncing each consonant distinctly. Speaking too quickly leads to slurred words and poor articulation, so slow down. Make a conscious effort to pronounce each word in the rhyme correctly.

Your pace impacts the clarity of your speech also. If you speak too quickly, your audience will have a hard time following you. But if you speak too slowly, you will bore them, and they will disengage. Your goal is to speak at a moderate pace and use pauses strategically. Pauses give your audience time to absorb your message and you time to collect your thoughts. Pausing before and after key points signals to your audience that this information is important (Gupta, 2023).

The best way to improve your speech intelligibility is to listen to yourself speaking, both in the moment and via recordings. If you have access to a recorded meeting from work, listen to yourself with your communications ally. Note when you aren't clear or your pacing needs work. Then, compare notes with your ally. You might also record yourself telling a story or giving a presentation you have practiced. Analyze your diction. Are there particular consonants or words that give you trouble? At what points do you speak too quickly or slowly? Are you speaking loudly enough to be heard? Or does it seem like you are shouting?

Action Plan

- **Tongue twister practice:** Choose two or three tongue twisters. Practice saying each one slowly five times for five days in a row. Choose different tongue twisters to practice for four weeks.
- **Record and listen:** Record yourself speaking and listen to the playback. Pay attention to your pace and identify areas where you're speaking too fast or too slow. Ask your communications ally for feedback. Practice adjusting your speed until you find a comfortable and engaging pace.

STRUCTURING YOUR THOUGHTS FOR CLEAR AND CONCISE EXPRESSION

Clarity leads to more effective communication. For introverts, structuring thoughts leads to more concise, impactful conversations. When preparing for presentations or important discussions, write your comments using bullet points and creating outlines. Doing this eliminates rambling and keeps you on point with a clear message. This streamlines your speech and allows you to focus on delivering each point with precision.

It's like preparing a grocery list before heading to the store; you're less likely to forget important items when you have a plan.

When it comes to speaking, effective speech structures play a pivotal role. Consider the classic three-part structure: introduction, body, and conclusion. Open with a captivating statement to grab attention, follow with detailed points that support your main message, and close with a memorable summary or call to action. This framework provides a clear path for both you and your audience to follow, reducing the likelihood of getting sidetracked.

Action Plan: Clarity

- **Structuring a discussion:** Write out bullet points or an outline for a product or improvement discussion. Record yourself discussing these points, then analyze the recording for clarity. Ask your communications ally or trusted coworker to listen and provide feedback. If you were unclear, redo your weak points, rerecord, and analyze a second time.

Precision in conversation requires eliminating filler words that clutter speech. Filler words, such as "um," "like," and "you know," often creep into dialogue unknowingly. They can distract listeners and diminish the impact of your message. Here's a list of common English filler words to limit or avoid:

ah, uh huh, hmm	well	totally
like	highly	literally
yeah	seriously	similarly
basically	actually	right
just	okay	so
kinda (thing)	clearly	alright

Filler phrases are just as bad. Please avoid the following and all their cousins:

you know (what I mean)?	I mean
sort of	at the end of the day
that being said	something like that
I want to say	for all intents and purposes
believe me	a little bit
I guess	

Precision also involves making smart word choices. Your vocabulary choices need to reflect the level of intensity you want to express. It's like choosing to label an art piece "pretty," "very beautiful," or "stunning."

Speaking of "very" in English, it's best to avoid it when possible. Instead of saying "very happy," replace it with the more precise word "ecstatic." "Very angry" could easily turn into "furious," which also drops one word, making it more concise. In the same way, something that is "very small" is "tiny." A thesaurus can be your best friend to find more precise synonyms for expressions using "very."

When you speak, you need to adapt your speech's conciseness to the level of the audience's understanding. Take this example from Chapter 1 about brain science: "In the frontal lobes and anterior thalamus—areas associated with deep thinking and planning." Both refer to the same part of human anatomy. People with medical backgrounds or biology teachers would likely know the placement of the "anterior thalamus" and its function. If you are non-medical, the important distinction is that it's a brain part "associated with deep thinking and planning." Neither description is incorrect. But they target different audiences. As you grow as a more effective business communicator, your word choices will increasingly adapt to your auditors until you become an introverted wordsmith.

Action Plan: Precision

- **Self-analysis:** Write down several sentences you've recently used at work. Identify any filler words you should eliminate. Practice out loud rephrasing these sentences with fewer interruptions.
- **Improved versions:** Record yourself delivering these improved sentences while making an effort to speak more succinctly. Critique yourself and get the input of your practice partner to arrive at clearer and more concise sentences. Pay special attention to your word choices. Did you use the word "very"? What could you have said instead?
- **Sales pitches:** Prepare a clear and concise sales pitch, technical product, or process explanation for two very different audiences. Speak them out loud until your communication ally says your delivery sounds authentic and natural without filler words or poor word choices.

THE INTROVERT'S GUIDE TO PERSUASION

> *Words are sacred. They deserve respect. If you get the right ones, in the right order, you can nudge the world a little.*
>
> — TOM STOPPARD, BRITISH PLAYWRIGHT AND SCREENWRITER (FAJÍN-RIVEIRO & MITCHELL, 2024)

"Persuasive introvert" is not an oxymoron. You can be very persuasive. But many of us introverts haven't had many opportunities to sound enthusiastic, confident, and powerful. Introverts don't often get the chance to speak. Analytical introvert Jason Stinnett identifies missed windows of opportunity as a key reason introverts fail to persuade (Stinnett, 2018). In our fast-paced culture, extroverts usually speak first and loudest while our introverted brains are still processing our responses. If your inexperience makes you feel insecure, thankfully, you can remedy this situation. You can adjust your presentation through practice until you feel and sound secure, just like the tourist who asked a local how to get into Carnegie Hall. The New Yorker replied, "Practice, practice, practice" (Lynette, 2018).

Quiet Brilliance Consulting (Lynette, 2018) proposes this exercise, which requires 5–10 minutes daily to help you sound and act poised: Choose a song, speech, or piece of poetry that you find moving and energizing. It should be short enough that you can read it over at least twice in five minutes. Stand tall, like you have a string attached to the top of your head pulling you up. Your feet should be apart, and your shoulders relaxed. (You're now in a Power Pose.) Pick out an audience in your mind, someone supportive and friendly who would like to hear your message.

Speak out your selected piece slowly. Emphasize the important points by slowing down, but not to a crawl, and lowering your tone. Alternatively, you may speak more loudly to add emphasis. Varying your pace and voice tones prevents you from sounding monotonous and dull. Don't let your voice drop when you end phrases or sentences, as that sounds dreary or tired. Pause to check your posture about halfway through. Be sure you are taking deep breaths also instead of breathing shallowly. Read your piece aloud at least three times or for five minutes minimum (Lynette, 2018).

After a few days, graduate to giving your piece in front of a mirror to practice making eye contact with your imaginary listener. Doing so moves you from reading to connecting with your audience. Then, work on projecting your voice by moving your listener progressively further away from you. Say your piece to your communications ally or a friend asking for feedback. The next week, move on to a new piece and repeat the cycle.

After you've done your preliminary work to get your voice and persona ready to persuade, move on to the question of how you will persuade. The answer: Not like an extrovert. "How you persuade as an analytical introvert looks nothing like how a salesperson does it" (Stinnett, 2018). Your persuasion style should look different because you have strengths many extroverted people don't have. Hype is probably not your thing, and that's fine. If you try to "sell," you won't be believable to those who know you. But your natural style gets the job done: exploring and presenting options and identifying and being transparent about potential problems (Stinnett, 2018).

You sound confident. You've committed to persuading like an introvert. Now, you must grasp the psychology of effective persuasion. Psychologist Robert Cialdini nailed down six well-known principles of persuasion. You can think of them as categories for people's motivations (Psychology Today Staff, n.d.).

They are:

- **Reciprocity:** People feel the need to give back to someone who provided a product, service, or information.
- **Scarcity:** People want items that they believe are in short supply.
- **Authority:** People are swayed by a credible expert on a particular topic.
- **Consistency:** People strive to be consistent in their beliefs and behaviors.
- **Likability:** People are influenced by those who are similar, complimentary, and cooperative. People are swayed by those they like.
- **Consensus:** People tend to make choices that seem popular among others.

At its core, persuasion is about understanding the motivations that drive both the audience and the speaker. Because you excel at observing and analyzing, you have a significant introvert advantage. Imagine a moment when you need to convince your team to adopt a new strategy. Your colleagues might be skeptical and have both spoken and unspoken concerns. You don't yet know their different motivations. Herein lies the key: Each person's motivations are shaped by their fears, desires, and experiences. To convince them, you must unearth their motivations and address their unspoken concerns through active listening with open-ended questions and empathy. Once you've tapped into these motivations, you can craft your message in a way that resonates deeply.

Consider the case of introverted manager Gretchen, who successfully advocated for a flexible work schedule. By assessing her team's needs and presenting a well-reasoned argument, Gretchen won them over. Her persuasive power lay in her ability to align her proposal with the team's shared goals, demonstrating empathy for their work-life balance. Conversely, another introvert, Neide, struggled in a high-pressure sales pitch, which prized rapid responses. Her lack of preparation and understanding of her client's motivations led to a less persuasive outcome.

Learn your audience's motivations by stepping into their shoes, considering what drives them, and tailoring your approach accordingly. For instance, when addressing a skeptical client, highlight how your proposal addresses their specific pain points. For an efficiency task group, emphasize the streamlined processes your suggestion offers. In a team meeting where consensus is key, frame your ideas as collaborative solutions that benefit everyone. With customers, you can build trust by showcasing testimonials and proven results. When engaging with management, align your proposals with the company's long-term vision, reinforcing how your ideas contribute to shared success.

When it's possible, also tailor your communications to how your audience processes information to make your message more accessible to others. If you are speaking to introverts, don't lose them in the weeds by giving them too much information too quickly. They won't be able to process it and will get frustrated. Instead, deliver your message in bite-sized chunks with pauses to allow for processing time and questions. For example, explain non-complex problems in 1–2 sentences. Then, present your solutions using a format like this one:

I have two solutions I'll walk you through. *<pause for questions or clarification>* Here's the gist of Approach A and the top strengths and weaknesses. *<pause for questions or clarification>* Now, here's the gist, strengths, and weakness of Approach B (Stinnette, 2018).

This process beautifully removes you from the spotlight more often. You also can know if you've succeeded. When you hear your coworkers or clients explain the situation the way you did earlier, you've nailed it (Stinnette, 2018).

Reflect on your own experiences. When have you been most persuasive at work? Was it during a project meeting that you had time to prepare and align your message with the team's objectives? Or was it a one-on-one conversation where you could delve into the listener's perspective? Identifying these moments can reveal patterns in how insights from the psychology of persuasion affect your communication style.

Action Plan

- **Pitch:** Outline your pitch for implementing a new procedure at work or replacing one.
- **Audience motivations:** Identify three distinct audiences you interact with at work (i.e., a customer base, a task group, or a management team). For each audience, write down what motivates them. What are their needs, values, or fears? If you don't know their motivations, investigate.
- **Develop pitch:** Develop the skeleton of the above pitch for implementing a new work procedure. Your team is your audience. Write out your message word-for-word so you can

check it for clarity and conciseness. Insert pauses at the appropriate points.
- **Practice:** Practice your full pitch aloud 3–5 times. Record yourself for self-evaluation and ask your communications ally to critique you.

4

EMBRACING NONVERBAL COMMUNICATION

What you do speaks so loud that I cannot hear what you say.

— RALPH WALDO EMERSON (BLOCH, 2015)

A bustling conference room, with its myriad of silent conversations, is a place where words are only a part of the dialogue. Here, nonverbal communication takes the stage, playing an unsung yet crucial role. Body language includes physical movements and postures. This subset of nonverbal communication constitutes around 65% of our overall communication

(*The Role Body Language Plays*, n.d.). Other elements of nonverbal communication include facial expressions, tone of voice, and personal space. It's not just about what you say but how you say it—or rather, how you present yourself while saying it. Even the most eloquent speech can falter if betrayed by closed-off postures or wandering gazes.

Positive body language projects confidence and openness, while negative body language signals defensiveness or discomfort. Picture a colleague delivering a presentation with shoulders back and eyes meeting the audience. This posture exudes confidence and invites engagement. Contrast this with someone hunched over, arms crossed tightly. That posture screams discomfort or resistance and undermines the message they're trying to convey. In American negotiations, a firm handshake, coupled with direct eye contact, sets the tone for a successful business agreement. On the flip side, avoiding eye contact or fidgeting might signal uncertainty or lack of confidence, potentially jeopardizing the negotiation's outcome. This dynamic illustrates the power of nonverbal communication in influencing decisions.

Your body language can also impact how approachable you appear to colleagues and clients. Consider the difference between open and closed stances. An open stance signifies a relaxed, approachable body language: a warm smile, uncrossed arms, palms facing outward, facing the other person directly, leaning slightly forward, and maintaining good eye contact. People are naturally drawn to warmth, confidence, friendliness, and receptivity. You are willing to engage. Conversely, closed-off stances create barriers, making others feel unwelcome or ignored: crossed arms, slouching, averted gaze, avoiding eye contact altogether, or turning away. When you send these negative signals, your coworkers perceive you are unwilling to listen (Pollack & Pollack, 2024).

Be conscious of your nonverbal cues. Work to open your stances by uncrossing your arms and smiling. Strive for an upright posture that conveys authority and attentiveness rather than slouching. Turn to face people when you address them. Your improved body language will make your communication more effective.

In professional settings, misinterpretations of body language lead to misunderstandings. Especially in multicultural environments, a gesture or posture you view as innocuous might be perceived differently by your colleague or client. For example, consider a new Korean immigrant, Mrs. Cho, whose family just took over a convenience store. Black male Mr. Washington comes into the store and pays with a $20 bill. Mrs. Cho places his change on the counter in front of him, following her Asian practice of not touching strangers, especially those of the opposite sex. However, Mr. Washington is offended, thinking she is discriminating against him on the grounds of race (Tidwell, 2016). This misunderstanding illustrates how essential it is to be aware of these potential pitfalls and strive for clarity in your nonverbal communication. (More on cross-cultural communication in Chapter 11.)

Action Plan: Reflecting on Your Nonverbal Communication

- **Self-observation:** Spend a day observing your own body language at work. Note any patterns or habits you have. Pay specific attention to how you use your hands and your posture.
- **Feedback from peers:** Ask a trusted colleague to observe your nonverbal cues during a meeting and provide honest feedback.
- **Practice:** Choose one aspect of your body language to improve, such as maintaining eye contact or adopting a more open posture. Practice this consciously throughout the next month.

USING FACIAL EXPRESSIONS TO ENHANCE YOUR MESSAGE

Facial expressions can transform a mundane message into something engaging and memorable. Think of the last time someone smiled warmly at you during a conversation. A smile is not just about showing teeth. That simple act can convey approachability, breaking down barriers and inviting connection. Similarly, a raised eyebrow can add a dash of curiosity or skepticism, depending on the context. It's a subtle cue that shows you're engaged and interested, prompting others to share more. Mastering your facial expressions and learning to read others' faces will significantly elevate your communication game.

Aligning your facial expressions with your verbal content is key for ensuring your message lands as intended. Imagine discussing an exciting new project with your team, your words brimming with enthusiasm. If your face remains expressionless, the dissonance can confuse listeners, leaving them questioning your sincerity. Expressing enthusiasm through raised eyebrows, a bright smile, and animated eyes enhances your verbal message, making it more compelling. Similarly, aligning your tone of voice with facial expressions reinforces your message. A warm tone paired with a smile conveys friendliness, while a serious tone coupled with a focused expression signals importance. It's about creating a cohesive message where words and expressions work in harmony, minimizing the risk of misinterpretation.

Micro-expressions are those subtle, fleeting facial expressions lasting only 1/5th of a second. They reveal genuine emotions even when someone tries to hide them. For example, in high-stakes situations like higher-level negotiations, people may get emotional when they lie for fear of getting caught or because they feel guilty or ashamed about the lie. Watch for this involuntary emotional leakage. This might be why some individuals find it challenging to hold a "poker face" when playing cards. You must watch your counterpart's face intentionally to spot these quick moments or you will miss your opportunity to adjust your responses accordingly (Shen et al., 2012). Force yourself to look up from your screen.

Here are the most common micro-expressions and their American significations:

- **Disgust:** A scrunched-up nose and a raised upper lip.
- **Anger:** Tightened eyelids, lowered and drawn together eyebrows, and pressed together lips. In

more intense expressions, the jaw comes forward, and the eyes may bulge.
- **Surprise:** Dilated pupils, open mouth or dropped jaw, arched eyebrows, and wide exposed eyes.
- **Contempt:** Neutral eyes with the lip corner pulled and stretched back on one side (7 Universal Facial Expressions, n.d.).

Cultural differences can add another layer of complexity to facial expressions. In some cultures, maintaining direct eye contact is seen as a sign of confidence and honesty. In others, it is disrespectful, confrontational, or full of sexual innuendo. A smile in one culture might convey friendliness, while another culture interprets it as insincerity. New immigrants or visitors may not yet pick up on your home culture's norms. If you have clients or work with colleagues from a culture not your own, google what eye contact and facial expressions (frowning, smiling, etc.) signify in their cultures. Learn what whistling signifies, too. If you travel internationally, be sure to do your homework so as not to offend your hosts. Armed with this information, you can prevent giving off unwanted vibes.

Action Plan

- **Self-analysis:** Look at recorded footage of your face during your daily business interactions. (Maybe from recorded Zoom meetings.) Make a list of your facial expressions or lack of them in relation to the conversation. Were your facial expressions appropriate?
- **Micro-expressions:** List any micro-expressions yourself or other people made in the recorded conversation. What did each micro-expression signify? How should you respond to this signal?
- **Practice:** In front of a mirror, work at developing a range of expressions. Make your welcoming face, your curious face, your questioning face, and the one you use to affirm others. Work daily on these expressions until they begin to come naturally.
- **Cross-cultural research:** Research the cultural norms regarding eye contact and facial expressions from the largest minority culture represented in your workplace or clientele. If possible, ask them what they find offensive. They'll appreciate your sensitivity.

THE IMPACT OF GESTURES AND POSTURE ON COMMUNICATION

How does a bored teenager sit? When you see your customers flailing their arms, what does it mean? What gesture does your boss use to communicate disapproval? How does someone with great poise like Britain's Princess Kate present herself? How would you describe her posture? What gesture does your favorite basketball player use to signify victory?

When used effectively, gestures can powerfully reinforce your verbal communication. They act like highlighters in a textbook, emphasizing key ideas and making them stand out. Making meaningful hand movements while you are speaking actually boosts your listeners' memory retention, too. Their brains will process both your speech and nonverbals together, making the message stick better (The Speaker Lab, 2024). In formal presentations, gestures should be deliberate and purposeful, enhancing clarity rather than stealing focus. Pointing to a specific area on a slide can draw attention to a critical statistic, or using an open palm can invite questions at the end of a presentation. These gestures communicate openness and confidence, inviting your audience to engage with you.

Inappropriate gestures detract from or destroy your messages. Does someone tap their pen on the desk or play with their hair when talking with you? Did someone "cheer" at another person's failure? That's a great way to kill empathy! While seemingly innocuous, nervous habits like twiddling your thumbs can distract others and undermine your professionalism. If you find someone's gestures annoying or offensive, make sure you aren't unconsciously making the same mistakes.

The appropriate space for gesturing is from the top of your chest down to the bottom of your waist. Gesturing outside of this imaginary box can be distracting or make you seem out of control. People appreciate smooth, fluid gestures rather than jerky or robotic ones that look unnatural or distressing. It's not that abrupt gestures, like raising your fist quickly, don't have their place to emphasize a point. But they should be used sparingly. Giving people the "stop" signal (flashing your palm at them) too often and finger-pointing can become offensive. Avoid crossing your fingers, too, as it implies you aren't sure something will work. Sexually charged or obscene gestures are off-limits. The middle finger isn't appropriate, even in jest, in business settings. Please, please keep your clean hands out of your pockets too! You can't gesture when your hands are hidden (Edwards, 2019).

Here's a list of appropriate American gestures you should be using:

- **Outward palms:** To emphasize a point or present an idea.
- **Upward motion:** To indicate growth, increase, or a positive trend
- **Downward motion:** To signify decrease, negativity, or a decline
- **"Boxing" motion:** To compare two options side-by-side
- **Encircling gesture:** To represent a whole concept or group
- **Thumbs up vs down:** Something good vs something bad
- **Meshing or folding hands together:** To signify coming together
- **Hands to chest vs. finger pointing toward someone:** Me vs. you
- **Using your fingers to count.**

A few common hand gestures are missing from this list because they are culturally charged. The "Okay" sign tells an American that everything is well or under control. But in Germany, France, and many African countries, it's vulgar and insulting. The peace sign made by holding your index and middle fingers in a "V" shape denotes peace, goodwill, or victory in America. But this gesture becomes rude in the UK and Australia if your palm is facing inward. Crossing your fingers is inappropriate in Vietnam. Don't point at statues or images of the Buddha with your index finger either (The Speaker Lab, 2024).

To improve your own gesturing, start by observing positive examples at work. Notice colleagues who consistently use gestures to strengthen their messages. Perhaps it's a manager who subtly nods while listening, signaling agreement, and encouraging further dialogue. Begin thinking of specific situations when you should employ positive gestures. Next, practice these gestures while speaking in front of a mirror until they appear natural and appropriate. Then, bring your smooth gestures to work with you.

Your posture profoundly influences how others perceive your confidence and professionalism. Your open stance, standing tall with your shoulders back, exudes authority and attentiveness, signaling to others that you are engaged and ready to contribute. Techniques for maintaining an upright posture include imagining a string pulling you upward or practicing yoga to build core strength and balance. If you tend to slouch, try incorporating these techniques into your daily routine. During meetings, periodically check your posture, ensuring you're presenting the most confident version of yourself.

While gestures and posture are powerful, overusing them can leave your coworkers frustrated. Excessive gesturing, including too many rapid movements, is distracting, not to mention tiring for your audience's eyes. Is there a colleague whose constant gesturing reminds you of an exercise routine? While this would be entirely appropriate in Italy or Greece, Americans would find it distracting, and the Chinese would see it as too informal or lacking respect (The Speaker Lab, 2024). If you have a tendency to "talk with your hands," check with an honest coworker to see if you are over-doing it.

Action Plan

- **Self-analysis:** Use recorded business conversations to write down your gestures and their contexts. Do you have a go-to gesture? Were your movements positive or negative? Did your hands stay within the gesture box? Were they too high, too low, or just right? Note areas for improvement.
- **Irritating gestures:** Ask your team members if you make any gestures that irritate them. Do

the same for any international workers in your sphere.
- **Positive practice:** Mimic positive gestures in front of a mirror, practicing until they feel natural. Invite your communications allies to give feedback, ensuring that your gestures enhance rather than detract from your message.
- **Posture:** Monitor your posture at work for a week. Note the number of times you slouch or use closed stances. Try to reduce that number next week. Repeat.

ALIGNING VERBAL AND NONVERBAL COMMUNICATION FOR CONSISTENCY

What would happen if your company president congratulated your team using a flat tone and deadpan expression? What if he had his hands in his pockets and never quite made eye contact? What would you think? How would you feel listening to him? Would his words seem like sincere compliments? Despite the clarity and strength of your president's words, their nonverbal cues tell a different story, one of discomfort and uncertainty. This misalignment between verbal and nonverbal communication leaves listeners confused about the speaker's credibility and sends unintended negative messages.

Consistent messaging, where verbal and nonverbal elements harmonize, is vital for effective communication. When your words and body language align, they reinforce each other, creating a cohesive message that is both believable and engaging. For example, when discussing a successful project, you underscore your speech by nodding affirmatively and maintaining eye contact. Doing this improves your outcomes. Conversely, if you speak with enthusiasm but maintain a closed posture, your audience may question the sincerity of your excitement.

To align your verbal messages with appropriate gestures, consider the context and content of your communication. For instance, when describing growth or expansion, using broad, open hand gestures can visually emphasize your point. In contrast, when conveying precision or detailing a specific point, more controlled, pointed gestures can help focus attention. Animated movements and an energetic tone of voice complement a passionate speech. "I'm so happy for you" needs a bright smile and an optional warm hug to appear genuine. These gestures should feel natural and complement the rhythm of your speech.

Consistent alignment in communication also builds credibility and trust. When your verbal and nonverbal messages align, you project authenticity, making it easier for others to trust you. Your tone of voice must match your facial expression and gestures. If you're expressing empathy, ensure your tone is gentle and your expressions soft. If you're conveying urgency, let your posture and gestures reflect that intensity. Feedback from your audience can provide valuable insights into how your message is received. Be open to adjusting your alignment based on their responses. If you notice puzzled looks or disengagement, reassess your delivery and make necessary adjustments.

Action Plan

- **Effective alignment:** Choose two recent interactions you deem to have been effective. What were you doing with your body and voice? Write down how your tone, gesture, and posture were aligned. Write down a situation where you might employ that combination again.
- **Non-alignment:** Choose two recently failed interactions. Were there conflicting signals between your words and your nonverbal cues? Identifying these moments. How were you perceived by your listeners? Write down what changes are necessary to align your verbal and nonverbal cues. Practice the same interaction

with correct alignment until it becomes second nature.
- **Role play:** Rehearse scenarios together where alignment is crucial, such as delivering a proposal or handling a difficult conversation. Pay attention to how your verbal and nonverbal cues interact. Get your ally's feedback on how to make your messaging more consistent.
- **Adjusting:** If your nonverbals and words become misaligned, ask your ally to respond with puzzled or disinterested expressions. This will give you opportunities to make quick adjustments based on feedback. Have your ally stop you if you don't pick up the signals. Take a moment, if you need it, to think about how to align your message. Then continue.

5

ENERGIZING TECHNIQUES FOR INTROVERTS

After an hour or two of being socially on, we introverts need to turn off and recharge ... This isn't antisocial. It isn't a sign of depression.

— JONATHAN RAUCH (RAUCH, 2003)

Bustling networking events are filled with chatter, clinking glasses, mingling, and the inevitable small talk. If it's an evening event after a full day at work, your energy for interactions might already be waning. The truth is introverts have a limited reservoir of social energy that must be managed carefully to avoid feeling depleted. Like a smartphone that needs daily recharge, you, too, require specific strategies to maintain your energy levels throughout the day. Marti Olsen Laney, author of *The Introvert Advantage*, says introverts resemble rechargeable batteries. You "need to stop expending energy and rest in order to recharge. This is what a less stimulating environment provides for introverts. It restores energy" (Olsen Laney, 2002).

Recognizing what drains your energy is the first step in managing it effectively. In an office environment, multitasking is the norm. You're juggling emails, phone calls, and meetings, all while trying to focus on that critical report. It's a classic case of spreading yourself too thin, leading to mental exhaustion. Research shows that multitasking, particularly for introverts, can be less effective and more draining than focusing on one task at a time (*Balancing Your Time and Energy as an Introvert*, 2018). This is because multitasking splits your attention, preventing you from delving deeply into any one task (i.e., using your reflective superpower).

High-energy social events are another common energy drain. Think of the company party where the music is loud, tableware is clanging, and everyone seems to be talking at once. Such environments can suck the energy right out of you. It's not that you dislike socializing. It's just that the high stimulation can be taxing. Similarly, certain interactions can leave you feeling drained. Even well-meaning colleagues can sap energy, especially if they tend to dominate conversations or require constant attention. It's not that you're disinterested in their grandkids or new car. You just want to finish your hors d'oeuvres.

On the flip side, recognizing what boosts your energy can transform your day. Starting your morning at home with a quiet moment and a latte could set a positive tone for your workday. Or, you could take just a few extra minutes in the shower after a workout. This quiet time allows you to mentally prepare for what's ahead, gathering your thoughts in solitude. During the workday, creating small pockets of peace can be revitalizing. Some introverts find solace in short walks, a few moments of deep breathing, or simply closing their eyes for a brief respite. Such breaks can recharge your batteries, providing a much-needed pause amid the chaos. But you must be intentional in establishing these rhythms.

After work, engaging in activities that genuinely interest you can replenish your energy, allowing you to unwind and refocus. Whether it's reading, gardening, or even a bike ride with a low-key introverted friend, these moments of personal time are crucial for recharging. Don't diminish the importance of self-care. Both your personal and professional lives benefit from it. It's like plugging in your phone overnight, ensuring you're fully powered for the next day's challenges.

Action Plan: Identifying Your Energy Influencers

- **List your energy drains:** Reflect on your typical work week. Identify activities, environments, and interactions that leave you feeling exhausted. Are there tasks that could be streamlined or delegated? People with whom you should limit contact?
- **Energy boosters:** Identify what activities or practices boost your energy. Consider what you do at home before work, during your workday, and after work. How can you integrate more of these into your routine?
- **Action plan:** Mark your calendar to dedicate time to activities you love twice a week. Give yourself 5–15 minutes of "you time" before work (maybe after you've gotten the kids off to school or childcare). Choose one activity to practice at work to renew. Then, practice consistently for three weeks to form a habit.

STRATEGIES FOR RECHARGING QUICKLY

It's 3 p.m. You had back-to-back product development meetings that lasted three hours this morning, and that extra shot in your lunch expresso just isn't cutting it. Your brain feels like it's liquifying. But you need to focus on correcting that annoying programming glitch holding everyone up. Your boss has already stopped by multiple times to "encourage" you to work quickly. You need an energy recharge, and you need it now!

How can you recharge quickly and efficiently?

Let's start by giving your brain the oxygen it craves. Breathing exercises are a quick fix for low energy. When stress hits, our breathing often becomes shallow, depriving the brain of much-needed oxygen. You can reset your nervous system by consciously taking slow, deep breaths. Try the 4-7-8 technique coined by Dr. Andrew Weil: Inhale for four seconds, hold for seven, and exhale for eight. It's like giving your brain a gentle nudge, reminding it to relax and recharge. This practice can be done anywhere—at your desk, in a meeting room, or even during your commute. It's an invisible tool, always at your disposal (5 *Breathing Exercises to Tackle Anxiety*, 2023).

Next, let's move your body. Sitting for long hours can lead to fatigue and discomfort. Remind your body that it's not a statue. Desk stretching exercises are a great way to recharge. Movement, even small, is key to staying energized. By practicing simple stretches at your desk, perhaps rolling your shoulders or stretching your arms overhead, you can relieve tension and boost circulation. If you need more specific ideas, check out these two short YouTube videos: "Five Stretches At Your Desk (Without Getting Up)" by Back Intelligence (Back Intelligence, 2019) and "Daily Desk Stretches - Stretches to Do at Your Desk to Prevent Pain" (Dare To Be Active with Dr. LA Thoma Gustin, 2019).

Moving into your mind, you can meditate. A short meditation session, even five minutes, can refresh your mind and calm your nerves. Picture yourself in a quiet room, eyes gently closed, focusing on your breath. This simple act can reduce stress, clear your mind, and infuse you with a sense of tranquility. You don't need a special mat or a serene garden. You can meditate in a quiet office corner or even your parked car or the bathroom stall.

Alongside these techniques, consider incorporating micro-breaks into your routine. These are brief, intentional pauses that allow you to step away from your tasks and refresh your mind. They might seem insignificant. But micro-breaks are incredibly effective in maintaining energy. Give yourself a hydration break. Look out the window. Do a quick eye exercise like the 20/20/20 rule: Look at something 20 feet away for 20 seconds every 20 minutes (*Wellness Wednesday*, 2020). Taking a moment to step outside for a breath of fresh air can be revitalizing. The change of scenery, coupled with the outdoors, acts as a natural energizer. Alternatively, a brief walk around your office floor can invigorate your senses, providing a quick mental reset.

These strategies are not just about managing energy but optimizing it. They empower you to take control, ensuring your energy reserves are replenished throughout the day. As you incorporate these techniques, remember that energy management is a personal journey. What works for one person might not work for another, so feel free to experiment and discover what recharges you best.

Action Plan

- **Breathing:** Set a timer for 30 seconds. Do the 4-7-8 technique until the timer goes off: inhale for four seconds, hold for seven, and exhale for eight.
- **Desk stretches:** Choose three desk stretches to try. Set a 3–5 minute timer. Do stretches until the timer goes off. Be sure to stretch your neck and shoulders. Set a daily reminder to do office stretches.
- **Meditation:** For those who already do yoga, bring it to work by doing a 3–5 minute meditation session to recenter. If you haven't

meditated before and can find a quiet enough location, try meditating for 2–3 minutes.
- **Micro-breaks:** Choose two micro-breaks that get you away from your desk. Do one in the morning and one in the afternoon. Even if you choose other options, be sure to hydrate multiple times during the day.

MAINTAINING FOCUS DURING PROLONGED MEETINGS

In the marathon of business meetings, maintaining focus can feel like an uphill battle. It's not that we introverts aren't interested. But cognitive fatigue sets in when our brains are constantly vigilant, processing information. It's akin to running a mental marathon without the luxury of a pit stop. Our minds can become weary from the barrage of data and dialogue. This exhaustion isn't just mental. It leads to sensory overload. The constant hum of voices, the flickering of presentation slides, and even the air conditioning's drone become overwhelming distractions.

A few preparation steps can minimize slumps during meetings. The first is to watch what you eat. Hunger pangs from skipping breakfast won't help you focus. Your lunch especially matters for afternoon meals. Fatty meals can push you into a post-lunch dip much faster, while eating carbs boosts energy and alertness. Eating healthy snacks mid-meeting should keep you energized. Doing something active right before the meeting also arouses your brain. Taking the stairs and having a cup of Joe can activate both your body and mind.

Minimizing your meeting distractions can prevent early meeting slumps. Start by choosing your seat carefully, avoiding windows and doorways. You want a position where you will be more engaged with your fellow participants. If you are well engaged, you won't lose your attention as quickly. You need a clear view of the speaker. Usually, the best spot is in the middle of the table.

Fortunately, the University of Plymouth released a study that shows doodlers retain 29% more information than others. Unconsciously, your brain remains more active when you doodle, keeping you out of a meeting slump. If you think others will be suspicious, share the joy that doodling can help them stay focused, too. Be sure to include your boss in the loop, especially if said person is old school. Have fun doodling ATVs, animals, flowers, or swirls while you retain important information and keep your mind actively engaged (*Overcoming a Meeting Slump*, 2020).

Another tactic is active participation through questions, which stimulates cognitive engagement and keeps you alert. By engaging with the material, you signal to your brain that this is a dialogue, not a monologue. Ideally, pull out the questions you formulated when you went over the meeting agenda to see if they are addressed. If not, interject them when appropriate. If the discussion doesn't permit you to ask your question, write it down as an action point for following up on the meeting. Doing this not only maintains your focus but also contributes to the meeting's productivity.

Implementing small mental breaks during lengthy meetings also enhances your ability to stay present and engaged. Pause briefly to stretch or take deep breaths to give your brain the oxygen it craves. Practicing mindfulness techniques, such as focusing on your breath or the feeling of your feet on the floor, can ground you in the present moment. This focus sharpens your concentration.

Reflecting on past meetings can provide valuable insights into your focus patterns. Consider two recent meetings: What went well, and what could have been improved? Perhaps you found yourself drifting after the first hour or losing interest when the conversation veered off-topic. Next, identify strategies to enhance your focus next time. Maybe it's sitting closer to the speaker to minimize distractions or setting specific objectives for your participation.

Continuing with the themes from our discussion in Chapter 2, setting personal meeting goals can also enhance your engagement. Before each meeting, define what you hope to achieve. Are there key takeaways you want to note? Contributions you'd like to make? By setting intentions, you provide your mind with a roadmap, guiding your focus throughout the meeting. Write out your intended contributions, even if they are more questions than statements. This preparation can serve as a mental anchor, keeping you engaged and proactive.

Action Plan

- **Reflection:** Think through your reactions during the past two marathon meetings. When or how far into the meeting did you first find yourself drifting? What sights or sounds distracted you? Were you yawning (which is your brain crying for oxygen)? Write down the following: distractions, what went well, questions you could have asked, and two things you will do differently next time.
- **Prepping:** For the next marathon meeting, choose two possible locations where you would

like to sit to minimize distractions. Plan some mental break times for when your focused attention wouldn't be as critical, like when the speaker may go over very familiar material.
- **Goals and questions:** Look over the agenda. Write out what you want to get out of the meeting. (clarification for a work assignment? putting a new idea on the table?) Write out your intended contributions, including questions. Practice saying your contributions and questions aloud 3–5 times.
- **Meeting time:** Write down the discussion's key points. Write down the answers to your questions. Write down action items you must complete. Take a deep breath once or twice. Push your feet into the floor to ground yourself. Decide if you picked a better location for maintaining focus. Why or why not?

SETTING BOUNDARIES TO PROTECT YOUR ENERGY

You've gotta keep control of your time, and you can't unless you say no. You can't let people set your agenda in life.

— WARREN BUFFETT (*A QUOTE BY WARREN BUFFETT*, 2024)

It's the middle of Tuesday morning. You're in the zone, concentrating deeply on a new design project that demands your full attention. Suddenly, your coworker interrupts with an unrelated request from production. It's a seemingly small disruption. But it pulls you away from your flow, leaving you feeling drained and frustrated. Also, it's not the first interruption of the day. This scenario highlights the importance of setting personal boundaries, especially for introverts who need to protect their energy reserves to maintain balance. Boundaries act as a safeguard, preserving your mental space and helping you navigate the demands of professional life without succumbing to exhaustion. Setting healthy boundaries is an act of self-care, not selfishness.

Consider a positive example of boundary setting: Project manager Mike has a strict no-meeting policy during designated focus hours. By communicating this boundary clearly with his team, he ensures uninterrupted time for deep work, resulting in higher productivity and job satisfaction. On the flip side, Sean struggles to say no, often agreeing to take on extra tasks at the expense of his well-being. Over time, Sean gets burned out, impacting both his mental health and work performance. These examples illustrate the profound impact that boundaries, or the lack thereof, can have on your professional life.

Communicating boundaries can be challenging, as you must assert your needs without feeling guilty. Our introverted tendency is to say "yes" to avoid conflict and keep others happy, often at our own expense. You can maintain boundaries guilt-free by framing your needs positively and emphasizing the benefits for both parties. For instance, you might say, "I need some quiet time to focus on this project to ensure I meet the deadline." This approach not only communicates your boundary but also highlights your commitment to quality work.

Wording boundaries can be tricky. But these three strategies can help: When you need to communicate "no," buy yourself time if you are caught off guard. A simple "Can I get back to you? I need to check my schedule" gives you breathing space. When your answer should be a firm "no," try sandwiching your refusal between two positive statements: "Thanks for thinking of me. Sadly, I don't have the bandwidth to take that on currently. I appreciate your understanding." Sometimes, you can offer an alternative: "I'm sorry, but that meeting time won't work for me. Can we meet over coffee this afternoon?" Just be sure not to offer alternatives every time, as it leads to overcommitment. You can say "no" without being rude or antisocial. Don't be afraid to respect yourself (*The Quiet Power of Saying No*, 2025).

Here are some other great strategies from Ashley Janssen (2021):

- Set fixed focus blocks on your calendar. Let your colleagues know these are interruption-free periods.
- Incorporate open/interruptible blocks into your work schedule.
- Ask your team members to group all their questions together and bring them to you during the above scheduled open office hours.
- Have your coworkers ask themselves the following questions before interrupting you: How urgent is my question? Can I work on

something else while I am waiting to have my questions answered? Can this issue wait until the open hours period?
- Have your team members bring a list of the solutions they've already tried before they bring the problem to you.
- Triage interruptions from most urgent to least urgent. Only emergencies and the most pressing matters merit a phone call or personal visit outside of open hours. The next tier down should handle matters via a text message with a 10–20 minute turnaround time, followed by a chat you would answer within a few hours, or an email within 24–36 hours.

Balancing flexibility and firmness in boundary setting is an art. While you must protect your energy, being too rigid can hinder collaboration and growth. Assess situations to determine when flexibility is appropriate. For instance, ask yourself, "Is my immediate input required, or could I offer it in writing? What is the priority for my workload right now?" If your supervisor requires your presence at a team meeting that is scheduled during your focus time, you probably need to flex and adjust your schedule temporarily. An honest discussion with your superior about the best ways to protect your focus periods might also be in order. If so, stress how protecting your optimal work periods ultimately benefits you both.

When your boundaries are challenged or ignored, it's important to respond constructively. Reinforcing boundaries assertively can prevent future infractions. For example, if a colleague repeatedly interrupts your work, remind them of your need for focus time. You might say, "I value your input. But I need to stay focused during this block of time. Let's connect in two hours." This statement reinforces your boundary while maintaining a collaborative tone. Sadly, you may need to be firm in handling boundary violations with certain people. They may need to hear your firm "no" three times before they take you seriously. Hold your ground. You are worth it!

Ultimately, you are your own bottom line when it comes to setting and maintaining boundaries. No one else can do it for you, and it takes consistent practice. You may need to deprogram yourself from being ON all the time. You do NOT need to be accessible at all times. Don't let yourself be cursed by "immediacy." The world will go on if you don't respond within three minutes. Lose your phone or put it on "Do not disturb" for certain time periods. Overextending yourself indefinitely is unsustainable. It leads to burnout and/or the cycle of overwork, sickness, recovery, and repeat. Take Warren Buffett's advice and take control!

Action Plan

- **Knowing your limits:** Reflect on situations where you feel overwhelmed or stretched too thin at work in the last few weeks. Write down what factors caused the situation, being as specific as possible. Is this situation repetitive? Write down the boundary you need to set in place for each instance. (Example: I will only accept calls from Sam once a day.)
- **Communicating boundaries:** Craft two possible scripts for setting boundaries respectfully. One might be addressing a chatty coworker: "I enjoy our conversations. But I need a block of quiet time to concentrate this afternoon." Another could be for a manager who frequently assigns last-minute tasks: "I'm happy to help. But I'll need advance notice to fit it into my schedule." Practice saying your "no" scripts in front of a mirror 3–5 times. Then, practice with your communications ally.
- **Boundary violations:** Write down boundary violations in the past two weeks. Brainstorm on how to address these issues moving forward. Write down 2–3 ideas to address these

situations. (Do you need to communicate with your supervisor? Have a firm conversation with someone?)

- **Flexibility vs firmness:** Write down three work scenarios in which your boundaries should be inflexible. Write three different boundary scenarios where flexibility is a possibility. Specify the conditions in which you might flex.

CREATING A PERSONAL WORK RECHARGE PLAN

Introverted people who balance their energy have perseverance and the ability to think independently, focus deeply, and work creatively.

— MARTI OLSEN LANEY (KANE, 2023)

Crafting a personal recharge plan is akin to designing your very own oasis amidst the bustling chaos of daily work life. It's your conscious plan to weave moments of tranquility and rejuvenation into your schedule so that you function optimally. The first step is to pinpoint key times throughout your day that naturally lend themselves to focused work vs breaks. Consider the rhythm of your workday. When do you do your best work? Are there moments when you naturally feel a dip in energy? When do you feel hungry? If coffee breaks aren't already part of your work schedule, would a mid-morning or mid-afternoon time be appropriate for a pause? You can strategically plan short breaks that align with your body's natural cycles by identifying these windows.

After you have picked specific break times, try incorporating sensory relaxation into your recharge plan to enhance its effectiveness. Music plays a significant role. Compile a playlist with calming tunes or nature sounds that help you unwind. Visuals, such as serene images or calming colors, can also be integrated into your workspace to give you a visual respite from your digital screens. Aromatherapy can be a subtle yet powerful tool. A few drops of lavender oil on a handkerchief or a woody-scented candle at your desk can create a calming atmosphere, soothing both mind and body.

Finding or creating quiet zones is another essential component of your recharge plan. You need a retreat zone where you can step away from the noise. This might require a bit of creativity in an open-plan office. Is there a quiet corner in a nearby park or maybe a less-frequented area in your building that could become your sanctuary? If physical space is limited, use noise-canceling headphones to carve out a personal quiet zone, even amidst the hustle and bustle.

Once you've identified these elements, it's time to write out your recharge plan. First, list the key times you've identified for breaks. Choose a sensory element or two you plan to incorporate, whether it's a specific scent, playlist, or visual aid. Describe your quiet zone and how you'll utilize it. This written plan becomes your guide, providing a clear structure to follow. As you implement the plan, pay attention to how each element affects your energy levels and adjust as needed. Perhaps you'll find that a particular scent invigorates rather than soothes or that certain times are more conducive to breaks than others.

In a month, re-evaluate your plan. Reflect on what worked and what didn't, and tweak it accordingly. Continuously refine your recharge plan, ensuring that it evolves to meet your changing needs. Remember that this is a personal endeavor. What works for one person might not work for another, so embrace the process of discovery. It's not about rigid adherence but rather flexibility and adaptability. If you are consistent for at least 3 weeks, this plan can become an integral part of your routine.

Action Plan: Your Work Recharge Plan

- **Recharge times:** Choose two or three possible recharge times of varied lengths.
- **Sensory additions:** Write down a potential sensory aid for your sight, hearing, and sense of smell that you can incorporate into your routine. Write down your favorite snack options for taste and something tactile you can manipulate with your hands (i.e., stress ball). Purchase what you need.
- **Quiet zones:** Choose one or two locations to which you can retreat.
- **Retreat:** Mark your calendar and retreat three times per week, preferably for 15–30 minutes daily.
- **Evaluate:** Monthly adjust your recharge plan as needed. Did they start a construction project next to the park? You might need to select a new location. Did that scent make you too invigorated? Change to a different one.
- **Unplug:** Do not connect digitally during your breaks. Give your eyes rest from screen time.

6

ENHANCING DAILY WORKPLACE RELATIONSHIPS

I didn't want to lose my sense of myself in my profession.

— MARISSA MAYER *(INSPIRING MARISSA MAYER QUOTES TO GET YOU THROUGH THE WORK DAY, 2017)*

Vulnerability is the birthplace of innovation, creativity and change.

— BRENÉ BROWN (WALTERS, 2014)

Authenticity lays the groundwork for genuine connections and trust. It's about showing up as yourself and fostering an environment where others feel comfortable doing the same. This doesn't mean airing every personal detail but rather integrating your true self into your professional persona. As an introverted professional true to yourself, you must balance self-assurance and humility. When colleagues see you as genuine, they're more likely to open up, share ideas, engage fully, and be loyal. Your commitment to authenticity creates an environment where trust can flourish.

Authenticity also means being self-aware and taking responsibility for failures. Transparent people are upfront and truthful about their limitations. They are honest about their flaws and vulnerable about their past. Warren Buffett called buying Berkshire Hathaway his biggest mistake, "a 200-billion-dollar mistake" (Sizemore, 2013). Oprah opened up about her childhood traumas. Their examples highlight how embracing vulnerability builds authenticity. This is not about sharing every insecurity but rather acknowledging that no one has all the answers. It maintains professionalism and relevance rather than oversharing. You ask for help when needed and admit when you don't know something. If you are open about your own challenges and uncertainties, people will trust and respect your honesty.

Globally, the business environment is becoming increasingly cynical and distrustful. In business communications, honesty is no longer enough. People are looking for authenticity which respects others as much as self. Per communication expert Nick Morgan, the new definition of authenticity means "expressing yourself in a way that is true to your values, but also sensitive to the context and needs of your audience." You must balance being transparent with being thoughtful about how your message will be received (Holt, 2024). Authentic communication is a two-way street. Take your listener(s)' temperature. Are they feeling disconcerted about upcoming downsizing? Or are they excited about a new project? If you find the project frustrating, don't pretend to be overjoyed. Audiences detect fake emotions in a heartbeat.

Sharing personal insights is a powerful way to build rapport. It invites others into your world, creating a sense of shared humanity and emotional connection. Talk about a challenge you've faced or humbly share a success you've achieved, finding moments where personal experiences intersect with professional goals. For example, share how your childhood interest in puzzles led to a career in problem-solving. Your puzzle-loving self makes you more relatable to colleagues. These insights go beyond mere words; they are invitations to connect on a deeper level.

Throughout this discussion, I've implied something that merits being stated plainly: Someone who balances authenticity and professionalism treats others well. This person respects coworkers and is concerned for their well-being. Gossip, slamming other team members, and nitpicking are off the table.

Action Plan: Embracing Authenticity in the Workplace

- **Inauthentic moments:** Write down a time when you didn't feel authentic at work. What went wrong? What do you think caused it? (fear of vulnerability? trying to be an extrovert?) What change(s) can you make to prevent this from happening again?
- **Identify authentic moments:** Reflect on a recent workplace interaction where you felt true to yourself. What made that interaction feel authentic? How did it impact your relationship with your colleagues?
- **Personal insights:** Think of a personal story or experience that shaped your professional journey. Jot down the details or write them out to practice being concise. Practice saying it aloud more than three times. Tell it to your communications ally. Plan to share this in an upcoming meeting or casual conversation.

- **Your needs:** Write down three things you don't know or understand at work. Write down two problems you are having. Practice saying them out loud. Tell them to your communications ally. This will make introjecting them into conversation more natural.

SMALL TALK AND BEYOND

If you find yourself cringing at the thought of discussing mundane topics like the weather or weekend plans, you're not alone. Most introverts dread small talk because it often fails to create meaningful connections. But it serves a purpose in the workplace. Small talk acts as a social lubricant, easing the transition into more substantive conversations. It sets the stage, allowing you to gauge the mood and dynamics of the room, making it easier to navigate into deeper conversations. Understanding its place can transform how you engage in it. Small talk doesn't have to be shallow; it can be your gateway to meaningful dialogue. The key is to approach small talk with the mindset that it's merely the opening act, not the main event (Helgoe, 2013).

Introverts who are successful at small talk don't talk about controversial topics: politics, social issues like civil rights, ethics, and sometimes tech (cryptocurrency,

AI). They don't interrupt conversations but wait for lulls and verbal cues to engage. They're not egocentric. Even the thought, *No one would want to talk with me,* focuses on self. It's not about you, though you might share something personal. Introverts who have mastered small talk know it isn't entirely about the other person, either. No one wants to feel interrogated. Instead, strive for a balance between what you ask and what you share.

Here are a few other helpful small talk preliminaries: Don't use slang. If you aren't speaking your first language, speak more slowly and focus on good enunciation. Since you don't want to waste the other person's time, give the person your full attention; put your phone or tablet away. Before you approach someone, have a fully formed question in mind. You don't want to interrupt and then have nothing to say. Start with an icebreaker: "Hey, do you have a few minutes to talk?" Then, launch your question. Maybe, "How has being in this new team changed things for you?" or "What would make this project better?" (Contributor, 2021). Be concise (think back to our discussion in Chapter 3).

Small talk stays on the surface. But these simple strategies can transition it to more meaningful dialogue. One effective technique is to ask open-ended questions that encourage expansive answers rather than "yes" or "no." Questions like "What inspired you to pursue your current career?" or "What projects are you most passionate about right now?" invite the other person to engage by sharing their thoughts and experiences. Try using "why" questions that invite more detailed responses. For example, instead of asking, "What did you do this weekend?" you might ask, "Why do you enjoy skiing?" This subtle shift encourages the other person to share more about their motivations and interests and builds rapport (King, 2020).

In addition to asking open-ended questions, genuine curiosity is essential. Showing a real interest in others deepens your relationships. Pay attention to the underlying themes in conversations. If a colleague often mentions frequent trips or loving a certain region, you might follow up with, "I noticed you enjoy traveling. What's been your favorite destination and why?" This demonstrates that you're listening and valuing their input. Open yourself up to learning from the other person. Each individual brings unique experiences to the table and unfamiliar perspectives. Sharing personal insights also fosters reciprocity. You can share knowledge and refine your skills together (*12 Tips to Have Better Conversations in the Workplace*, 2024).

Action Plan

- **Small talk openers:** Write out five small talk openers, such as, "Why are you passionate about your current role?" or "Why do you think our team works so well together?" Next, create two mock dialogues using these openers, imagining how the conversation might naturally evolve. Practice them with your communications ally.
- **Questions:** Jot down five questions that encourage deeper engagement. Make them specific to your environment if possible. For instance, "What do you enjoy most about working in our industry?" or "How do you think our team can improve?" Practice them with your communications ally.

IMPROVING WORK CONVERSATIONS

Leveraging your active listening skills and empathy goes a long way in improving your interactions on the job. But, you must first put the preliminaries in place to elevate your conversations to the next level. Start by clearing the airwaves, so to speak.

Each of us has prejudices and biases. It's part of our human condition. However, our preconceived notions can undermine our work conversations if we are not careful. It's imperative that we stop ourselves from making assumptions, even those based on past experiences. These predictions about what the other person thinks, feels, or needs often result in misinterpretations of that person's actual messages. Instead, work actively to step into work dialogues with a clear, open mind, ready to explore new ideas and solutions. Strive to understand the other person's perspective, asking questions to clarify your own understanding. You just may learn something new about the other person.

Next stop: multitasking. Give the conversation your full attention as a sign of respect for the other person, even if they don't reciprocate. Your undivided attention prevents you from missing key information. When you are looking at your tablet, you miss important body language cues and microexpressions. If you're distracted, you might also take longer to respond, which disrupts the conversation's flow. Be fully present if you're serious about improving as a communicator.

Each person has opinions and different perspectives, anticipates differences, and handles them respectfully. When conversations begin degenerating, draw on your sense of empathy to stop the downward spiral. Disagreements do not have to be distasteful. Instead, pay close attention to what the other party is saying and acknowledge their feelings, even if you disagree.

Seek common ground, areas where your objectives and/or values might align. Work toward middle-ground solutions or compromises. Stay calm and be kind. Your demeanor sets the tone for your next conversation with that person (*12 Tips to Have Better Conversations in the Workplace*, 2024).

Learning when and how to end conversations will reduce your stress and conserve your social energy. By showing respect for others' time, you preserve relationships, too. People will be happy to see you again if you keep your interactions friendly and concise. In terms of the conversation's content, work conversations often revolve around an objective like passing on knowledge, making a decision, or seeking input. Once the objective has been met, the interaction can end. Participants revisiting the same points or not finding anything new to discuss also point to finishing the conversation—nonverbals like checking the time, signs of distraction, or displaying restlessness signal a need for closure.

Sadly, certain chatty individuals don't pick up on the cues or choose to ignore them. Thankfully, conversations normally contain natural breaks or pauses. Even dominating extroverts run out of breath eventually. Seize these brief silent moments to wrap up the discussion without frustrating or belittling another person. Summarizing the discussion or gently mentioning your time constraints also helps: "I need to jump back into my report now." Or, you might outline your next steps: "Thanks so much for your time. I'll send a follow-up email with details." By staying positive and polite, you succeed. "Have a great day" is a perfect and safe happy ending for your interactions, especially if you smile when speaking. Thank all parties for their time also (*12 Tips to Have Better Conversations in the Workplace*, 2024).

Action Plan

- **Common ground:** Choose one or two of your coworkers. Write down 1–3 things you have in common, including possible work objectives (i.e., finishing a project) or relationship values (i.e., you both love your kids or you both value honest communication).
- **Different perspectives:** For the same people, write down two points at which their perspectives differ from your own about your work environment. It could be something simple, like different preferences for the color scheme, or more complex, like the best way to achieve a goal. Then, write down either their feelings on the subject or why their perspective has value.
- **Conversation endings:** Write down two phrases you can use to politely end

conversations. Be sure to express gratitude. Practice saying these phrases aloud multiple times.

- **Role-play:** Have a conversation with your communications ally. Begin with small talk before asking an open-ended question to engage deeper. After 3–5 minutes, conclude the conversation using one of your practiced endings from above.

Make a Difference with Your Review

"We rise by lifting others."

— ROBERT INGERSOLL

Because you're reading <u>The Introvert's Guide to Successful Business Conversations</u>, you recognize how impactful honing your communications skills can be for your personal and professional life. By now, you're beginning to leverage your introverted superpowers to excel in your verbal communication. You are practicing proven strategies, breathing exercises, and developing your toolbox of conversation starters, empathetic questions, and more.

What if you had embraced your introverted superpowers earlier? How much easier would picking up on nonverbals have been if you had found this book sooner? How has reading this book made work communication less intimidating and more effective? Would you recommend this book to a fellow introvert?

That's why your review matters.

Many introverted professionals just like you are searching for ways to navigate business conversations authentically. They want practical skills and tools to communicate with confidence on the job. Your review could help them find this resource.

Most people choose books based on reviews. Leaving one takes less than a minute. But your quick review can help another introvert to ...

- Discover their introverted superpowers.
- Speak up in meetings without anxiety.
- Connect meaningfully.
- Turn awkward small talk into valuable conversations.

To help, simply scan the QR code below and leave a review:

Please seize this opportunity to pay it forward by helping another introvert grow. Your kindness encourages me too. Thanks so much!

Avery Harper

7

HANDLING ON-THE-SPOT INTERACTIONS WITH EASE

You're on task and diligently focused on a budget analysis. Your manager abruptly appears and requests that you lead an impromptu meeting in five minutes. The sudden requirement to think on your feet can send a wave of anxiety crashing over you. Your mind races. You've been crunching numbers all morning and didn't prepare for this immediate pressure to be both articulate and insightful. What will you say?

For introverts who thrive on preparation and reflection, these moments can feel particularly challenging. They can leave you feeling exposed and vulnerable as if your mind has temporarily deserted you in your hour of need. It might feel like being thrown into a pool without knowing how to swim or being asked to solve a puzzle without seeing all the pieces. You're not alone. Many professionals face similar challenges when it comes to spontaneous interactions.

Realistically, you will be confronted with a litany of spontaneous speaking situations, both professionally and privately. In business, spontaneous speaking is much more prevalent than planned speaking engagements like presentations. They inevitably occur in meetings, hallway conversations, and even during casual encounters with colleagues. The key lies in developing strategies to navigate them with poise and confidence (*Be Better at Spontaneous Speaking*, n.d.).

THE PAUSE BEFORE YOU SPEAK

When you're caught off guard, it's natural to feel unprepared. Don't rush to answer. You need to move out of reactive mode. It's okay to gather your thoughts. Here are three strategies to help you buy time. All three overlap with the reframing below:

- **Pause:** It's perfectly appropriate to give yourself a few seconds to gather your thoughts. Give yourself permission.
- **Paraphrase:** Put the speaker's request or question into your own language, giving approximately the same amount of detail. Since

paraphrasing is a lower-order cognitive skill, it allows you the mental space to simultaneously engage your higher-level cognitive skills like brainstorming, creative thinking, problem-solving, and evaluative thinking.
- **Ask a clarifying question:** This will allow you to gather more information, better understand the situation, and make your response more relevant.

Do yourself a favor by creating a small time buffer. Remember others understand being in impromptu situations as well and offer grace. They realize you haven't had time to ponder or thoroughly prepare. Most often, they are calling on you because they know you already possess knowledge and valuable insights. They want what you have to offer, even if there are hiccups in your presentation (*Excel in Spontaneous Conversations*, 2024).

REFRAMING

Often, our initial reaction to unexpected interactions is to see them as obstacles, challenges, or threats. However, by consciously reframing these situations as opportunities, you can shift your perspective, reduce anxiety, and enhance your performance. Reframing doesn't mean you should ignore potential challenges. Instead, you are changing the narrative. This mental shift encourages you to engage more positively. Imagine being asked to lead a discussion on short notice. Instead of focusing on all the potential negative scenarios, consider it an opportunity to showcase your insights and leadership skills. Or, imagine being asked to provide feedback on a project with which you're unfamiliar. Rather than viewing it as daunting, see it as a chance to learn and contribute a fresh outsider perspective.

To illustrate, let's delve into an anecdote from a fellow professional. Introverted project manager Sarah was caught off guard when her team requested her input during a spontaneous brainstorming session. Initially flustered, Sarah took a deep breath, reminding herself that her insights were valued. She acknowledged the challenge, "This is an interesting topic; let me gather my thoughts." During her buffer pause, she organized her thoughts. Drawing from her expertise, she replied, "My initial thoughts are… But I need more time to evaluate how this proposal will impact…" Sarah made a thoughtful contribution. At the same time, she deferred to her introverted preference for deep thinking as an important follow-up step to the brainstorming session. In doing so, she gave herself permission not to have a thorough, quick response, which was entirely appropriate. It also communicated that she cares about her work.

In these moments, remember that authenticity is your ally. Rather than striving for perfection, focus on being genuine and true to yourself. Your unique viewpoint is a valuable asset, and your contributions are important. This shift in thinking allows you to focus on the value of your contribution rather than the fear of judgment. Engaging in these interactions becomes a chance to showcase your unique insights and perspectives, even if they aren't delivered with the polish of a prepared speech.

Action Plan: Reframing

- **Reflection:** Reflect on two impromptu interactions you experienced last week. In retrospect, what opportunities did each interaction present to you? Write down the opportunities (speak from your experience, learn something new, make a new plan, etc.).
- **Improvement:** Write down a positive action for how you would handle each of the above interactions differently now (give yourself a pause, ask a specific question before responding, and not take yourself so seriously, etc.).

BREATHING EXERCISES TO STAY CALM AND COMPOSED

The ability to stay calm and collected may feel elusive when you are faced with impromptu conversations. When your anxiety rises, your breathing often becomes shallow, exacerbating feelings of panic and unease. By consciously slowing your breath, you can signal your nervous system to relax, creating a sense of calm. As you gather your thoughts, try pursed lip breathing: with your mouth closed, inhale slowly for two counts. Then, pretending to whistle, exhale slowly for five counts. Repeat this five times. Or you could try equal breaths: inhaling through your nose for five counts, then exhaling through your mouth for five counts, repeating until your calm returns. Revisit the 4-7-8 breathing technique from Chapter 5: Breathe deeply through your nose for four counts, hold your breath for seven counts, and exhale slowly through your mouth for eight counts (*5 Breathing Exercises to Tackle Anxiety from Your Desk*, 2023).

If you have already incorporated breathing exercises during non-anxious moments of your daily routine, you will be able to access these calming techniques more easily when you need them most.

Breathing exercises aren't just about calming your nerves; they also give you a momentary pause to reflect. This pause can be crucial in spontaneous interactions, allowing you to transition from a reactive to a more thoughtful state. Imagine being in a situation where a colleague suddenly asks for your opinion on a complex issue. By taking a deep breath, you create a buffer between the stimulus and your response, giving you time to process the information and respond effectively. This practice can transform your approach to spontaneous interactions, allowing you to engage with clarity and confidence.

Action Plan

- **Breathing exercises:** Set an alarm to practice structured breathing for five minutes 3–5 times a week, including one time during your work commute. Do either 4-7-8 breathing, equal breaths, or pursed lip breathing. Keep practicing until these exercises become second nature.

QUICK THINKING AND ADAPTABILITY SKILLS

Navigating the unpredictable waters of spontaneous conversations calls for quick thinking and adaptability. Both are skills that can be cultivated with practice and intention. You already possess one of the most powerful tools at your disposal: active listening. Active listening in spontaneous conversations involves a few key techniques. You've already encountered the first technique: focus on clarifying questions. Ensure that you fully understand the other person's message. This might involve asking, "Can you elaborate on that point?" or "What do you mean by...?" When you ask such questions, you demonstrate that you are engaged, in addition to getting the information you need to respond thoughtfully.

Another useful technique is summarizing key points before you respond. A summary is slightly different from a paraphrase. When paraphrasing, you restate what someone is saying in your own words, aiming to cover most of the details. But a summary condenses what the speaker said into a shorter version focusing on the main points. As an example, note the three texts below:

- **Original text:** "The study found that regular exercise can significantly improve mental health."
- **Paraphrase:** "Research indicates that consistent physical activity has a positive impact on psychological well-being."

- **Summary:** "Exercise has been shown to greatly benefit mental health."

When summarizing, you might lead with something like, "So, what I'm hearing is..." You affirm your understanding and create a bridge to your own contribution. This step doesn't just clarify; it also buys you a moment to organize your thoughts and allows you to slow down the flow of the conversation from rapid-fire to the pace needed for reflection.

Sometimes, the response just isn't there. Don't fret. Saying "I don't know" just proves your honesty. You also show you don't operate on hunches. It can be a powerful move. But you need to follow it with, "But I'll find out/think about it and get back to you." When you follow through, you boost your credibility and build trust (*Excel in Spontaneous Conversations*, 2024).

Action Plan

- **Toolbox:** Make a list of clarifying questions and sentence leads that you can draw on during spontaneous interactions. These might include, "Could you clarify what you meant by...?" or "I understand that you're concerned about... Is that correct?" or some of the above examples.

Practice these responses until they become second nature.

- **Practice impromptu scenarios:** Make a list of likely impromptu scenarios you might encounter in your professional life. These could range from unexpected questions in meetings to sudden requests for feedback. Once you have your list, ask your communications ally or a trusted colleague to practice with you.

8

COMMUNICATING WITH AUTHORITY FIGURES

Okay, stay calm. You've thought this through, and you know your idea has value. Start by thanking her for her time. That's polite and sets a good tone. Then, get to the point quickly; no need to over-explain upfront. Just say, "I've noticed a way we could improve our customer onboarding process, and I'd like to share it with you." She'll probably ask for more details, so be ready to explain how it works and the benefits. But keep it concise. If she asks questions you're not prepared for, just say you'll follow up with more information. She's not expecting perfection; she'll appreciate your initiative. Just breathe. You've got this!

How do you move from being apprehensive about speaking with your boss to carrying on the above mental dialogue before your meeting?

Let's explore the unique pressures that come with interacting with superiors, especially when your manager seems unapproachable. You want to make a good impression, so there is the fear of negative evaluations. Take performance evaluations, for example. They can turn even the most confident individual into a bundle of nerves. You might worry that your words will be misconstrued, your intentions misunderstood, or worst of all, your capabilities questioned. This fear often stems from the high stakes attached to these interactions. After all, your boss holds a significant sway over your career trajectory. But remember, fear is not an insurmountable barrier. If you've worked at building rapport through your consistent performance and authenticity (look back at Chapter 6), you've already laid a good foundation for evaluations.

Intimidation is perhaps the most common emotion when facing superiors. The power dynamics in these relationships can amplify feelings of vulnerability. It's easy to feel dwarfed by the authority your boss represents, especially if they have an assertive personality. You might find yourself questioning the validity of your contributions or second-guessing your worth. However, it's important to recognize that intimidation is often a self-imposed barrier. Your contributions are valuable, and your perspective is needed. The key is to approach these interactions with preparation and confidence, bolstered by the knowledge that you are an integral part of the team.

Balancing assertiveness with respect is another intricate dance in the realm of upward communication. It requires finesse and practice. It's essential to remember that assertiveness isn't synonymous with aggression. As an assertive person, you respectfully and confidently state your needs and ideas clearly while maintaining openness to feedback and collaboration. This balance is crucial in ensuring that your voice is heard without alienating those in positions of authority.

Action Plan: The Empowered Communicator

- **Your boss(es):** What is your superior's communication style? Is this person affirming or pushy, friendly or withdrawn? What is the best way to give your boss feedback? (Consult with your coworkers if you need input.) Which of your coworkers interacts the most effectively with them and why? What can you learn from their actions?
- **Self-evaluation:** Think of two recent encounters with your superior(s). Write down how you reacted in each situation. What went positively? What didn't go well? What were you feeling and why? Do you have any internal

default emotional settings when you interact with this person? What would you like to see changed?

- **Performance evaluation:** You are being evaluated. Role-play your performance evaluation with your ally or a coworker who's already been through your company's procedure. Ask your ally/coworker to give you both positive and negative feedback. Record this exercise so that you can see your nonverbals and check your tone of voice.

BUILDING RAPPORT WITH AUTHORITY FIGURES

Building rapport with workplace authority figures is like tending a delicate garden. It requires patience, attention, and a genuine desire to understand and connect. Finding common interests or professional goals is a powerful starting point. You can pick up ideas through small talk, examining their office space, checking their social media, or asking directly. Imagine your boss enjoys sailing, and you share an interest in the serenity of open waters. This shared interest can become a conversational bridge, a way to engage them beyond the confines of work. Even if your interests don't align perfectly, finding common professional goals can achieve similar rapport. If your boss is driven by innovation, aligning your communications and projects with this vision demonstrates your commitment to shared objectives, fostering a sense of camaraderie.

Expressing appreciation for your authority figures can also deepen your relationship. But it requires subtlety, consistency, and sincerity. Forget overt flattery, even if your boss likes to have their ego stroked. A one-off accolade can appear disingenuous. Instead, draw on your empathy superpower. Cultivate the habit of complimenting your coworkers on their strengths and good work. They'll appreciate your encouragement and mutual respect. This practice also builds positivity within you and can be an antidote for complaining. Then, when you do express appreciation to your boss, it feels like a natural extension of your communication style rather than a calculated move. Focus on specific attributes or actions you genuinely admire. Perhaps your boss has a knack for remaining calm under pressure. Expressing gratitude for how this calm impacts you or sets a great example reinforces rapport and builds the foundation for good future interactions.

Action Plan

- **Common interests:** Write down 2–3 things that interest your boss, including one outside work pastime or hobby. What does your authority figure value at work? Do you have anything in common?
- **Compliments:** Write down sincere compliments for 3 to 4 coworkers. Practice these compliments and then deliver them. Write down a sincere compliment for your boss. Practice it and give it at the appropriate moment.

STRATEGIES FOR EFFECTIVE UPWARD COMMUNICATION

Work authority figures typically have several people reporting to them. They are busy, and their bandwidth is limited, just like yours. To set your messages apart, they must be clear, insightful, and aligned with your team's goals. Apply everything about precise communication and preparation from previous chapters with greater care in your upward communication. You must distill your thoughts into concise, impactful statements that convey exactly what you mean without leaving room for misinterpretation.

Consider the scenario of Aaron who approaches his manager with a lengthy, convoluted explanation of a project delay. At the end of the explanation, the manager has not obtained any clear, concrete information. Contrast this with Aaron articulating the core issue in a few succinct sentences: "Our supplier delayed shipment by two weeks, impacting our timeline. I've contacted them, and they're expediting the order. I'll update you by Friday." This transformation illustrates the power of clear, focused communication, ensuring your message is understood the first time.

Notice the "I" statement in the above comment. How you word your conversations with authority figures sends implied messages as important as your intended communication. When addressing your superiors, using "I" statements rather than "you" statements shows you are taking responsibility. It makes your conversation less emotionally charged and more neutral. When you couple "I" statements with qualifying words like "perhaps" or "maybe," rather than absolutes like "always," "all the time," and "never," you help diffuse their personal defenses or resistance (*Tips for Communicating Effectively With Your Boss*, n.d.).

Aligning your communication with organizational goals shows that you understand the bigger picture and are not just focused on your immediate tasks. Clearly identify your company's overarching goals, whether they aim to innovate in their industry, enhance customer satisfaction, or streamline operations. Then, pinpoint your department's specific objectives. If you're unsure of these objectives, don't hesitate to ask. Inquiry shows initiative and a commitment to contributing meaningfully. This extra effort demonstrates your strategic awareness.

Employers value foresight. Anticipating potential questions and concerns is akin to playing chess, where you must think several moves ahead. Before meeting with superiors, reflect on what they might ask. Consider the questions that have come up in past meetings. By preparing responses in advance, you not only appear confident but also demonstrate forethought. Once you've crafted your responses, let some time pass and revisit them with fresh eyes. This pause allows you to refine your answers, ensuring they're as comprehensive and effective as possible. Then, practice saying them aloud.

After a productive conversation, following up with a recap email can reinforce what was discussed and agreed upon. It serves as a record for both parties, maintaining clarity and accountability—practice writing a concise recap email after your next meeting with a superior. Summarize key points, decisions made, and any action items. If your supervisor appreciates such follow-ups, send it their way. Otherwise, keep it for personal reference to remind yourself of the discussion and ensure that nothing slips through the cracks. These strategies form the backbone of effective upward communication, enabling you to engage with authority figures confidently and with clarity.

Action Plan

- **Goals:** Write down your company's and department's goals. Incorporate specific time frames if they are appropriate. Review these goals at least yearly.
- **Preparing questions:** Write down two or more questions your supervisor asked you in the last month. Do any of them require follow-up? If you anticipate hearing the question again, write out your response. Review it and practice delivering it with your communications ally to ensure it is clear and concise.
- **Recap email:** Recap your last meeting with your supervisor via email. If enough time has elapsed, indicate your progress toward completion of your action items. Send the email if appropriate.

HANDLING REJECTION AND FEEDBACK WITH GRACE

You've just left a meeting with your boss, and it didn't go as planned. You submitted a project you poured hours into, only to receive a lukewarm response and a list of changes. The sting of rejection isn't just emotional; it feels personal. It's like being handed a cold cup of coffee when you were expecting a warm, frothy latte. How you respond in this moment can set the tone for your professional growth. Your next words and actions are key. A defensive response might close doors. However, approaching the feedback as a learning experience can open new pathways.

Handling your emotions in the moment can be challenging. You must balance accepting your emotions and displaying them appropriately. You can't ignore the sting and should allow yourself to feel disappointed or frustrated. But you also must guard against letting your emotions take control. Practicing emotional regulation techniques strengthens your emotional resilience for the times when control is critical. Do deep breathing exercises to calm the immediate physiological response to stress. This simple act can shift your reaction from knee-jerk defensiveness to thoughtful consideration. The breathing techniques for quick recovery from Chapter 5 and impromptu interactions from Chapter 7 work well in these situations, too. Take a deep breath, literally. It gives you time to think before you speak ("How to Handle Rejection Gracefully" n.d.).

Next, it's time to focus on your presentation. The more you practice observing yourself, the better you will become at controlling how you express your emotions. Pay attention to your stance, as you may need to open it and uncross your arms. A natural default to criticism is to tense and close up. What emotions are showing in your face? Are you frowning? Your goal is to relax and neutralize your body language, moving it from hostile to open. Work to manage your nonverbals so that your negative emotions stay out of your body language (International, 2024).

Check your voice as well. Your goal is to keep your feelings of anger and annoyance out of your voice. Your tone should be neutral, if possible. What is your default tone when you face rejection? How loudly or softly are you speaking? Do you sound angry? What is your pace? Are your words racing out of your mouth as fast as they are in your mind? Are you using any pauses? These delays give you time to regroup emotionally and intellectually. Observing how your boss responds to you can give good feedback on how you are doing.

Now, it's time to start reframing the rejection. To do so, you must view rejection as a part of the professional landscape. Obviously, that's harder when your boss says "you" in an angry tone. But you can choose to separate yourself from the rejection. If we see rejection as information rather than a personal attack, we can become more rational and make more informed responses. Change the problem into a challenge. Visualization can also help. Imagine the feedback as a stepping stone on your path, not a stumbling block. Each piece of criticism is a chance to refine your skills. Be kind to yourself and recognize that rejection happens to everyone. Self-care in the wake of rejection puts you back on track more quickly, so indulge yourself a little.

Developing a growth mindset can transform your upward communication. Seek constructive feedback from your boss. Doing so will boost your rapport greatly. Actively work to understand the reasons behind decisions and critiques. Ask yourself what you can take away from a particular rejection. You now have an opportunity to grow and develop new skills. Believe you can do better next time. By reading this book, you're actively working on self-improvement. Following through on rejection is just another step (how, 2024).

Developing a strong support network gives you a sounding board, providing perspective and encouragement when you need it most. Reflect on who is currently in your support network. Are there colleagues or mentors who offer constructive advice or a listening ear? Write their names down and consider who else could be added. Perhaps you have a peer in another department whose insights you value or a former boss who's always believed in your potential. These individuals can provide the encouragement needed to weather professional storms.

Action Plan

- **Self-assessment:** Write down two instances where feedback left you feeling deflated. Underneath each incident, make two columns. On one side, write down your responses, good or bad. In the opposite column, write what you should do differently next time for negative responses. Could you have taken more time to process before responding? Did you internalize the criticism, or did you manage to separate it from your self-worth? Look for negative patterns to address first.
- **Reframing:** For one of the above incidents, reframe the rejection by transforming it into a challenge. Write down two specific actions you can take to meet the challenge. These are your growth points.

- **Support network:** Write the names of people in your work support network. Write down the name of another person you can add. Next time a rejection occurs, contact one of these individuals just to vent a bit and be encouraged.
- **Role-play:** Have your communication ally call you out on something work-related (reject your idea, critique your performance, etc.). Record your interaction. Check your nonverbals. Repeat the scenario with your "boss" being more confrontational, so you force yourself to work harder to maintain emotional control.

BALANCING ASSERTIVENESS AND DIPLOMACY IN REAL TIME

Inevitably, you and your superior will disagree strongly at some point. Especially in instances of rejection, diplomacy asserts your position without overstepping the boundaries. In essence, balancing assertiveness and diplomacy in real time involves a blend of preparation, practice, and awareness. As previously mentioned, assertiveness is about expressing your ideas with confidence and clarity without resorting to aggression. Doing your homework to prepare and practice your arguments is a prerequisite to your success. Imagine you're in a meeting, and a decision is being made that you believe could negatively impact your department. Saying, "I think we need to reconsider the timeline to avoid potential pitfalls," asserts your perspective without creating unnecessary friction. It's about speaking your truth while maintaining respect and professionalism.

Diplomacy is about how you package your message to make it more persuasive or palatable. It isn't untruthful or manipulative. Instead, diplomacy expresses your opinion without offending your boss or coworkers. A frequent pitfall to this approach in real-time diplomacy is letting emotions take control, leading to hasty or reactive responses. The minute you offend or anger someone, they stop listening to you. You've lost them. The techniques for handling emotional triggers above apply here as well: Pause before responding, take a breath to regain composure, and think first. Consider a self-assessment of past interactions where diplomacy also faltered. What triggered the emotional response? How could it be approached differently next time?

How do you assert yourself diplomatically? Both your body language and verbal skills play into diplomatic responses. To prevent offending, you need to maintain a relaxed body language with an open stance. Inoffensive speech happens in a pleasant, light, subdued tone of voice. You must choose your words carefully. Bluntness rarely has a place in diplomatic speech. Instead, focus on understatement and expressing understanding. Avoid loaded words and phrases: wrong, too few, status quo, excessive, fortunately, favoritism. They imply judgment and pack emotional punches. Your goal is to reduce the emotion in your comments (Coles, 2023).

For times when your opinions differ strongly, using phrases to acknowledge and validate opposing views is key. Try saying, "I understand your perspective, and it's valid. Here's another angle to consider." Doing this respects their viewpoint while gently introducing your own. Instead of bluntly stating, "This won't work," a more diplomatic response would be, "I see the potential here. But I'm concerned about a few aspects. Could we explore some alternatives?" This approach invites dialogue and collaboration rather than defensiveness. Here are some more phrases to build your toolbox of diplomatic responses:

- **Agreeing:** "I completely agree with that point," "I'm on the same page with you," "I see eye to eye on this."
- **Disagreeing:** "That is a valid point, but" "I respect your point of view, but"
- **Suggesting:** "Why don't we," "How about"

Action Plan

- **Assertive statements:** Write three assertive yet respectful sentences you might use when communicating with a superior. Repeat them aloud, letting the words become second nature. Role-play these scenarios with your communications ally or a trusted colleague.
- **Failed diplomacy:** Write down two instances where you failed to be diplomatic. What triggered the emotional response? How could it be approached differently next time? Do you need to apologize? (Do so.) Revamp these interactions with your communications ally to help you improve your future responses.
- **Diplomatic sentences:** Write out 3–5 sentence openers you can use to acknowledge and validate opposing views. Practice saying them aloud to your communications ally.

9

MASTERING NEGOTIATION DIALOGUES

Everything is negotiable. Whether or not the negotiation is easy is another thing.

— COMEDIAN CARRIE FISHER (BBC BITESIZE, 2019)

Rather than going into specific negotiation techniques and jargon (i.e., BATNA, ZORA), this section focuses on using your introverted strengths to your best advantage in negotiations. You do yourself a disservice when you try to negotiate like an extrovert. Here's the good news: You don't have to change who you are to be an effective negotiator.

In negotiation, your active listening skills are a rare gift. Since listening is the only way to discover your counterpart's desires, needs, and fears, introverts get more information needed to strike win-win and long-lasting deals. Your empathetic listening skills make you come across as more sincere. That's a most welcome change since people are tired of being manipulated and fooled by stereotypical extroverted negotiators. Your authenticity comes into play with your substance-over-style approach, which builds trust. "No posturing, bluffing or confrontations are necessary" (*Why Introverts Are the Best Negotiators*, 2019). Being you works!

Introverts are skilled at paying attention to small details. For example, an introverted negotiator might pick up on subtle cues and unspoken concerns, allowing them to address the real issues. Or you might notice a hesitance and ask probing questions, uncovering that the other party is concerned. This attentiveness allows you to better understand the other party's perspective and craft effective responses tailored to their needs. Often, introverts also have strong analytical skills. You can anticipate likely scenarios and develop strategies to overcome potential obstacles before they are even voiced (Media, 2022).

Staying calm and collected is paramount to successful negotiation, and introverts often have the upper hand.

Your ability to be comfortable with silence can be a powerful tool, prompting others to fill the void with valuable information. Consider an introverted negotiator who approached a high-stakes business deal with a calm demeanor. Rather than dominating the conversation, she asked insightful questions, allowing her counterpart to reveal key priorities and concerns. This masterful technique not only provided her with valuable information but also positioned her as a thoughtful and strategic partner. Her quiet confidence and genuine interest in understanding the other party's needs led to a successful negotiation that benefited all involved. So, embrace your introverted strengths to become the best negotiator you can be.

Whether or not you've participated in a high-stakes negotiation, you're already encountering lower-pressure scenarios that occur daily. Think about negotiating project deadlines with a colleague, discussing resource allocation with a team leader, or asking for a raise. These situations provide excellent opportunities to practice and refine your negotiation skills in less intimidating settings. By approaching these interactions with the same attention to detail and empathy, you can build a foundation for handling more significant negotiations with ease.

Action Plan: Your Negotiation Strengths and Weaknesses

- **Reflection:** Who are the best two negotiators in your company or department? Write down what they do well. Who are the worst two negotiators? Write down what they do wrong.
- **Introvert superpowers:** Write down two ways you may have mimicked extrovert negotiators in the past. Then, write down two specific ways you will leverage your introverted strengths in the future (questions to a specific person, watching for a certain detail, etc.)
- **Self-assessment:** Write down 3–5 times you've had to negotiate at work during the past month. How did each situation turn out? How can you improve next time?

STRATEGIES FOR PREPARATION

A cardinal rule of negotiation is to foster relationships. Famed introvert and negotiator Warren Buffet has long mastered the art of negotiation. Authors Tom Searcy and Henry Devries have even written a book titled *How to Close a Deal Like Warren Buffett*. He is known for fostering good business relationships. At his company, Berkshire Hathaway, "building relationships is paramount… Buffett treasures long-standing partnerships based on mutual respect, not quick deals" (*MSN*, 2025).

Building a connection can transform the interaction from a transactional exchange to a collaborative dialogue. This rapport-building phase extends beyond a preliminary step throughout the entire negotiation and beyond. It's a continuous process which ensures that both parties feel valued and understood. Rapport-building questions foster a sense of trust and openness. Questions like "What inspired your interest in this project?" or "What challenges are you currently facing?" invite your counterparts to share more about themselves, signaling that you value their perspective. This sets a positive tone for the negotiation. You can further enhance rapport by performing background research on the other party via LinkedIn or the company's website to find out their interests. See what you can talk about to break the ice.

Law Professor Janice Nadler from Northwestern University School of Law also discovered that even a five-minute phone chat unrelated to the upcoming negotiation paid off for negotiators. Her research found these completely unrelated conversations primed counterparts to feel more cooperative, share more information, and make fewer threats than those who skipped the telephone small talk. "Schmoozing" and other forms of rapport-building create trust before substantive talks begin (Staff, 2024).

Key relationship building must be accompanied by preparation and planning. Warren Buffett meticulously researches and prepares for negotiations. He knows that every negotiation is different, even if the same people are involved. Buffett never relies on his gut or past experience—he studies (Overvest, n.d.).

Because this chapter isn't about how to meticulously craft negotiation plans, this is just a reminder to do your due diligence when preparing for a negotiation. Be sure to learn the other side's vocabulary in the process. This saves embarrassment later and earns your counterpart's appreciation (Staff, 2024). If Buffett needs to study, we all do. Put your introverted, analytical skills to good use as you develop your strategies and counter-proposals. You have what it takes to succeed.

Action Plan: Negotiation Preparation

- **Research:** Research your counterpart via social media or LinkedIn. Write down 3–5 rapport-building questions to discuss with this person. If it's your team leader, hopefully, you've already developed a rapport. Try to think of 3–5 new questions to ask him or her. Practice these questions with your communications ally.

- **Phone call:** Make that phone call to your counterpart and engage in 2–3 minutes of small talk with them. Take up to five minutes.

TECHNIQUES FOR EXECUTION

Though extremely important, preparation will not be enough for a successful negotiation. When you come to the table, you must present yourself as a thoughtful professional who cares about the other person(s) in the room. Your body language and tone should convey your respect for the other person and your willingness to engage in the negotiations together. Everything you learned about nonverbals in Chapter 4 applies here. Maintain eye contact, lean into the conversations, and smile.

Start by introducing yourself. It's so basic yet often forgotten. A simple "Hi. I'm Robin" works wonders. You'll earn more personal regard. Instead of being an annoyance, others present will see you as a fellow human being. Your smile and simple intro remind everyone around the table of the human element in play during the negotiation (Gaunt, 2021). Everyone wants to be recognized and treated fairly, so take time to discuss ground rules. Explain your style: "I am a conservative risk taker who prefers building trust over time" (Staff, 2024). Employing your empathy superpower is more than appropriate in bargaining.

Once the discussions begin, remember that the ultimate bargaining chip is knowledge, and a golden run of negotiation is to get as much information as possible from the other party. By letting the other person do most of the talking, you learn more (Latz, n.d.), Focus on gathering and analyzing what others are saying. Don't put unnecessary pressure on yourself to carry the conversation. Instead, apply the 80/20 principle: Actively listen 80% of the time and use the other 20% to speak. Focus on being a sounding board and information sponge. Ask open-ended questions (Media, 2022).

Be sure that your active listening includes these three key elements: paraphrasing, inquiry, and acknowledgment. Let's look at this example of Julian, a supplier of a component needed for a state-of-the-art new medical imaging device. Before the negotiation began, Julian submitted a written proposal to his manufacturing counterpart. Their buying rep points out two major objections: the price per unit is too high, and they need assurances the supplier's company can ramp up production if demand increases rapidly.

Below is a sample dialogue highlighting each element for a successful active listening response:

- **Paraphrase:** "It sounds as if you're satisfied with our component overall. But if I understand correctly, you need me to assure you that we can increase production if large orders come in. You're also concerned about our proposed per-unit price and our willingness to work with you to create an acceptable arrangement. Have I captured your main points?"
- **Inquire:** "You mentioned that you found our proposed price to be unacceptable. Help me understand how you came to this conclusion. Let's also talk about how we might set up a pricing structure that you find more reasonable."
- **Acknowledge:** "It sounds as if you're quite disappointed with various elements of our proposal, so much so that you have serious concerns about whether we'll be able to work together over the long haul" (Staff, 2024, October 1).

When it's your turn to speak, keep it simple. Knowing what you are asking for and why relieves your nerves and keeps things concise. Don't waffle or over-explain yourself, and don't argue. An offensive posture creates a negative atmosphere and doesn't equate to long-term results. Coupled with this, avoid making emotional bids. Keep your requests logical based on the research you did. Share the facts to make a reasoned, calm argument (BBC Bitesize, 2019).

Silence is a powerful tool in negotiations, too. Thankfully, your introverted self is comfortable with silence. Pauses give you time to gather your thoughts and assess the dynamics of the discussion. When faced with a challenging question or an unexpected turn, a well-timed pause prevents you from reacting impulsively. You create space to make your response more measured and impactful. Your silence can be interpreted as thoughtful deliberation, projecting confidence to your counterpart. Remember, silence can be as powerful as words. Embrace your advantages as an introvert: appreciate the pause, reflect thoughtfully, and think deeply.

Navigating aggressive negotiation tactics can be daunting. But your calm demeanor can diffuse tension and foster cooperation. Focus on the issue at hand and not the emotional drama. Suppose your counterpart adopts a confrontational stance, raising their voice or interrupting you. Don't panic. Pause, breathe, and take a moment to gather your thoughts. Don't mirror aggression. Otherwise, your dialogue may spiral into a vicious cycle. Maintain your composure and respond with measured, respectful language. This approach can shift the tone of the negotiation, encouraging a more collaborative dialogue.

Consider the following exchange: Your counterpart insists on an unrealistic deadline, leaving little room for discussion. Rather than reacting defensively, you might respond, "I understand the importance of a timely completion. Let's explore how we can meet those goals while ensuring quality." This response acknowledges their urgency while introducing an element of collaboration, opening the door for constructive problem-solving.

Realistically, not every negotiation has a happy ending. You can't control all the variables. Resuming dialogue at another time might be necessary. Or, it may need to end. But you haven't wasted your time. Look for the silver lining. Give yourself credit for what you did right and note where you should improve. If you succeeded in communicating your party's propositions clearly and understanding your counterpart's position, you've made your point and maybe even planted a seed for future collaboration. That deserves recognition (BBC Bitesize, 2019).

Action Plan: Negotiating

- **Asking for a raise:** Negotiate a raise with your communications ally. Record it to analyze your nonverbals afterward. Remember to smile; the camera is rolling!
- **Changing deadlines:** Your communications ally is your aggressive counterpart. Role play changing a deadline. Record the negotiations to evaluate your nonverbals afterward.
- **Three active listening responses:** Think of a recent negotiation. Write out your counterpart's objections. Then, write out your paraphrase, inquiry, and acknowledgment statement. Practice saying them aloud 3–5 times. Tell them to your communications ally.

IDENTIFYING WIN-WIN OUTCOMES

I won't fire you if you lose money, but I will if you lie.

— WARREN BUFFET TO GOLDMAN SACHS EMPLOYEES (OVERVEST, N.D.)

Negotiation need not be adversarial. Instead, it can become a conversation where preferences align rather than clash. The key is to see negotiation as a shared exploration of mutually beneficial outcomes rather than a zero-sum game. Achieving a win-win outcome is the gold standard for success. Introverts excel here, as their natural inclination to listen carefully fosters an environment of trust and goodwill. Take the case of Jade, an introverted product manager at a tech firm negotiating a partnership deal with a software company. Rather than approaching the negotiation with a hardline stance, she focused on building a rapport with her counterpart, an equally reserved but insightful lead engineer from the other company.

Their initial interactions were marked by mutual respect and quiet observation. Jade posed questions that delved into the engineer's goals and challenges. "What are the biggest obstacles your team faces in integrating new technologies?" This approach revealed potential areas for collaboration and also demonstrated her commitment to finding a solution beneficial to both parties. They discovered shared objectives, such as streamlining user experiences and reducing operational costs, and then framed the dialogue around these goals. In essence, they shifted the negotiation from a transactional exchange to a collaborative partnership.

The power of collaboration in negotiations cannot be underestimated. The potential for a win-win outcome increases significantly when both parties work together toward their shared objectives. The prerequisites are open communication and a willingness to explore creative alternatives. For instance, a product manager, Timothy, and an engineer, Ibrahim, brainstormed joint initiatives that leveraged each company's strengths. Their rapport allowed them to discuss potential roadblocks candidly and seek mutually advantageous solutions. Ibrahim appreciated the chance to voice his team's concerns. In turn, Timothy gained insights that informed his strategy. The resulting partnership expanded their market reach and enhanced their product offerings. This collaborative spirit met immediate needs and set the stage for future cooperation.

All of your introverted superpowers come into play to achieve win-win outcomes. Your active listening skills allow you to pay close attention to what the other party is truly saying. Your powers of observation let you pick up on subtle nonverbal clues. Your empathy builds trust and makes sure everyone is treated fairly. Your deep thinking and analytical skills might also lead you to generate a range of potential solutions. If you add to that practice and Warren Buffett's insistence on integrity, your negotiation skills will grow and shine. Tell the truth. Negotiations are about building relationships, and no company wants to deal with dishonest partners. Maintaining your reputation as a truthful negotiator is key. Remember Buffett's admonition (Overvest, n.d.).

Action Plan

- **Collaborative partners:** Write down a list of your company's partners, each party's contributions, and how each party benefits. Find out who negotiated the partnership to see how this person overcame any objections posed by his/her counterpart. Ask for negotiation tips if appropriate.
- **Collaboration questions:** Write down three questions you can use in negotiation that encourage collaboration. Include one that inquires about your counterpart's company needs.

10

STRATEGIES FOR CONFIDENT NETWORKING

Confident introverts don't avoid social situations. They just make wise choices.

— UNKNOWN

Networking events, often bustling with a mix of familiar faces and strangers, can feel overwhelming. Your introverted key to conquering this whirlwind lies in preparation. The next section focuses on your elevator pitch. But prep also includes setting realistic and achievable goals. Aim for quality over quantity. It's not about collecting a stack of business cards but about forging meaningful connections that are far more valuable. For instance, if you're attending a conference, set a goal to connect with three individuals who align with your professional interests. This approach not only makes networking more manageable but also more rewarding.

Research the event thoroughly. Familiarize yourself with the agenda, key speakers, and potential attendees. Identify two attendees you'd like to connect with, perhaps a speaker whose work you admire or an industry peer with shared interests. Prepare a few thoughtful questions to ask them, such as, "What inspired you to delve into this field?" or "How have recent industry trends influenced your approach?" This preparation fosters engaging dialogue and demonstrates genuine interest. Visit the location if possible. It's like walking into a room with a map—knowing the landscape empowers you to navigate it more confidently.

Go easy on yourself the evening before your networking event. You know that your introverted self needs solitude and quiet to energize. You also know that tomorrow's event will drain your social energy and could push you out of your comfort zone. Plan your "night before" accordingly. Attending any get-togethers or other functions that will deplete your energy probably isn't wise. Instead, do something that's proven to energize you. A bubble bath or man cave time may be in order. Apply this same principle after the event to recover more quickly. Life happens, but your goal is to build a cushion of time and space around each networking engagement (Autenrieth, 2018).

Two more preliminaries set the stage for your successful networking event. The first is to set a participation time limit of 30–45 minutes minimum. Even if you come to the event fully prepared, human interactions can be messy and awkward. You might experience a few false starts. You can give yourself an out, but only after you've picked up a drink or snack, tried to start a few conversations, and made an honest 30-minute effort to connect with others. Secondly, put away your phone before you go through the door. Hiding behind that virtual wall may be safe. But it prevents others from engaging with you and vice versa. You can check your Instagram Feed after you've met your 30-minute goal (Autenrieth, 2018).

As you step into the event, remember that your unique perspective as an introvert is a strength. Rather than forcing yourself to be extroverted, embrace your thoughtful, observant nature. Also, keep in mind that other people in the room have been dreading this event, too—maybe even some of the extroverts. The lump in your throat and the knot in your stomach are okay. You are not alone.

Everything you learned about small talk in Chapter 6 doubly applies to networking events. Exercise your active listening, nodding occasionally to show your engagement. When it's your turn to speak, respond thoughtfully, building on the other's ideas. Doing this creates a dynamic exchange rather than a one-sided monologue. Instead of the usual "What do you do?" consider opening with a more engaging question like, "What brings you to this event?" or "What are you hoping to learn today?" Reference the speakers or elements of the program. For instance, if a speaker's presentation resonated with you, mention it and ask for their perspective. This not only shows that you're attentive but also paves the way for a deeper connection.

About your business cards, please don't shower them on everyone around you. It's off-putting. Not everyone wants your card, even if they take it politely. Instead, only give them to the people you've conversed with quite a bit, like those you targeted in your preparation. Those you form a genuine connection with serendipitously probably will keep your card, too.

Action Plan

- **Role-playing:** Simulate networking scenarios with your communications ally or trusted colleague. Take turns initiating conversations, posing questions, and responding. Have your partner give you feedback on both your verbals and nonverbals.

ELEVATOR PITCHES

Picture yourself in the classic elevator pitch scenario: You're on the ground floor when the CEO of a company you've admired for years enters and pushes the 5th-floor button. You have just a few to make an impression. Your heart is pounding like a drum in a heavy metal band. But, unlike the characters in the late '90s movie trope, you don't stammer and bore the CEO because you've prepared the ultimate elevator pitch.

Developing elevator pitches is a topic much larger than the scope of this book. But you can apply your learning from previous chapters to leverage your introverted superpowers into composing and delivering your pitches. We're going to narrow in on pitching yourself rather than your company. Let's start with some stellar examples to illustrate just how impactful elevator pitches can be.

First, this young entrepreneur is introducing his startup: "Hi, I'm Alex, and I run GreenTech Solutions. We transform everyday waste into renewable energy, cutting emissions by 40% for our clients. We recently partnered with CityCorp, helping them save $2 million annually. I'd love to discuss how we can help your company achieve similar results." This pitch is golden because it's concise, highlights a clear value proposition, and includes a concrete achievement. It hooks the listener with its relevance and leaves them wanting to know more.

Now consider an artist seeking funding: "Hi, I'm Jamie, a digital artist creating immersive experiences. My recent exhibition, 'Ethereal Realms,' attracted 50,000 visitors and was featured in ArtWorld magazine. I'm looking for partners to expand internationally. Do you have a moment to hear how we can create magic together?" Jamie's pitch shines because it showcases their success and hints at future opportunities. It's engaging, memorable, and tailored to pique the interest of potential investors.

Contrast these with a less effective example: "Uh, hi, I'm Sam, and I work in tech. We, um, do a lot of cool stuff with AI, and, uh, yeah, it's pretty exciting. So, how about a chat sometime?" This pitch lacks clarity and purpose. It's vague, leaving the listener confused and uninterested. It highlights the importance of preparation and precision in writing a pitch.

Your elevator pitch is one of your most important assets because it describes your value (Wojnicki, 2023). When crafting it, your goal is to convey your expertise and unique selling points in a brief, impactful manner. Your pitch should contain a memorable hook, show your value, tell how you are different from the competition, and give a call to action. As you prepare, start by summarizing your professional skills and achievements in 2–4 sentences. Consider what sets you apart from others in your field. Perhaps you have led a successful project, saved your company money, or developed a new process. Work to capture highlights. If your job is multifaceted or you have expertise in multiple areas, write out different value statements for each of your skill sets. Evidence to back up your claims always adds value to your pitch, as in Jamie citing the 50,000 visitors to her exhibit above.

Developing a hook may seem intimidating. But your hook doesn't have to be fancy, complicated, or terribly creative. Simple and straight to the point are much better. The point is to spark the other person's interest. Speaking your audience's industry language and using your research data to point out their pain points builds credibility. Personal stories and statistics work well, too. For example, if your company is marketing an online collaboration tool, you could say, "73% of all teams will have remote workers by 2028" (Ramki, 2024).

Your call to action should push beyond just handing someone your business card. In the above examples, Jamie and Alex propose a meeting. Inviting someone to have a coffee chat might be appropriate for your contacts with the most potential. For others, you might ask them to connect with you on LinkedIn or share contact information. The key is to offer a follow-up opportunity without putting the other person on the spot.

Remember, clarity and brevity are your allies. The aim is to leave a lasting impression without overwhelming your listener with information. "Elevator pitches exist because humans have shorter attention spans than goldfish, and we really need a leg up on our aquatic competition" (Ramki, 2024).

If your elevator pitch is successful, questions will follow naturally. Anticipate them in advance and come ready with answers. During your preparation time, write down a few questions based on your research and pitch. What would your audience want to know? What might require further explanation? Your answers should go into more depth, providing more context.

But be mindful of other people's time, especially during networking events. Already you've extended an opportunity for conversation in your call to action. Don't monopolize your curious listener for 20 minutes on the spot. Set up a lunch meeting or Zoom call for later.

When tailoring your pitch to different audiences, consider their industry, the context, and the individual you are addressing. Are you speaking to a potential employer, a client, or an investor? Remember that your audience is a person who cares about something. Use your empathy superpower to focus on their interests as well as your own (Wojnicki, 2023). Each audience will have different priorities and interests, so adapt your language and tone accordingly. You do not want to deliver the same elevator pitch targeted at an investor to a potential collaborator. Likewise, different networking events may merit different elevator pitches depending on the event's audience.

A well-crafted pitch can fall flat if delivered without enthusiasm or conviction. You do need to practice with your communications ally or peer, especially monitoring your nonverbals. But be mindful of your audience. Elevator pitches can come off as impersonal or insincere when you have them "down cold." High-status people on the receiving end are aware of awkwardly memorized, self-promotional scripts. They've heard plenty before. Yes, you must know your pitch well enough not to stumble. But you're still addressing a human with whom you hope to establish rapport. Perfection and showmanship aren't as important as being your introverted, empathetic self (Wojnicki, 2023).

Action Plan

- **Selling yourself:** Write down your professional accomplishments, skills, and experiences. What are you most proud of? What feedback have you received from colleagues or clients? Now condense your notes into 2–5 sentences, each highlighting a different aspect of your value.
- **Pitch your company or service:** Do the same steps as above focusing on your company or a service they provide. Consider their collaboration partners, recent deals, new products, and so on. Be sure to use industry lingo and include helpful statistics.
- **Audience-specific pitches:** Write out three different pitches based on diverse audiences or settings. For example, prepare one for a networking event with potential investors, another for an event showcasing new industry trends, and a third for a career fair. Practice each one aloud three times. The third time,

record yourself and then analyze it. Share it with your communications ally to get feedback.

FOLLOW UP AFTER NETWORKING EVENTS

The networking event was a success. You made your goals, exchanged business cards, engaged in enlightening conversations, and even stayed more than 45 minutes. Now, you're back at the office with your business card collection. You shouldn't have more than 10. If your goal was to connect with three people, 3 to 5 cards is more reasonable. Remember quality over quantity from above. This is where the magic of follow-up begins. It's not merely a polite gesture; it's a strategic step in solidifying those initial connections and forging relationships. As the saying goes, fortune is in the follow-up. The key is to approach this with intention and authenticity.

Before leaving the event, take a moment to jot down quick notes about each meaningful conversation you had. It doesn't need to be elaborate. A few key words or phrases will suffice to jog your memory later. Something like "Anna—AI consultant—discussed industry trends" or "Mark—HR manager—interested in remote work policies" should be enough for your introverted powers of observation to fill in further details later. These notes will become invaluable in personalizing your follow-up messages. Ideally, you will follow up within 24 hours and won't need to reference these notes. But life happens, and the reminders can save you later.

Crafting personalized follow-up messages or emails demonstrates professionalism and courtesy. Start with an interesting subject line. (More on this below.) Then, address your contact by name and reference the event and the conversation you shared. This immediately establishes context and shows that you're not sending a generic message. As an empathetic communicator, think about what your contact would want to get from your message. For example, "Hi Anna, I really enjoyed our chat about AI trends at the conference. Your insights were fascinating, especially regarding the future of machine learning in healthcare." The second sentence gives a compliment, which is always appreciated. This personalization also creates a sense of familiarity and warmth, making the recipient more inclined to respond.

Your new contact likely receives 50+ emails per day, so you want your networking follow-up to stand out. Writing a brief and intriguing subject line increases the chances of your communication getting read. Try piquing their interest with the title of something they wrote, using their name, or noting a common interest.

"Subject: Maria, this may help with your sales goals" is a stellar example. It uses her name and offers her value. "Free for coffee?" isn't as eye-catching unless your new contact is a coffeeholic. But it gets the job done (Indeed Editorial Staff, 2024).

As you compose your message, be concise yet meaningful. Express your gratitude for the interaction and how you might benefit mutually going forward. If you discussed a specific topic, consider including a relevant article or resource that might interest them. Or offer to introduce them to someone of mutual interest. These elements add value to your follow-up and position you as someone who is knowledgeable and thoughtful. Suggest a follow-up action, such as a coffee meeting, proposing a choice of times. Offering a phone call option also acknowledges the other person's busy schedule. By proposing a concrete next step, you make it easier for your new contact to engage with you further.

Here's a great sample follow-up email taken from Indeed Career Guide (Indeed Editorial Staff, 2024):

Subject: Have you tried using WordLine to create your website?

Hi, Gabriel,

I'm glad we met at the Future IT event. I thought about our discussion on best practices for website development and loved your take on keeping up with the latest technology. Have you tried using WordLine? I use that framework for my website and found it user-friendly.

I'd love to chat more about it. Can we set up a face-to-face meeting next week over a cup of coffee? I'm available on Tuesday or Thursday morning.

Again, it was great meeting you at Future IT, and I look forward to meeting up soon.

Thanks,

Maya Smart

Maya's subject line was intriguing. She offered Gabriel value by introducing him to Wordline. She gave different meeting options. She also thanked him. To make her email even better, Maya could have hyperlinked her email to her professional online profile. That would have given Gabriel one more option to connect with her.

You are a professional. It goes without saying that your email must be clear and respectful. To make reading easier for your new contact, use standard fonts and sizes. Your email shouldn't be one long paragraph. Separate your thoughts into paragraphs. As always, run it through spell check or Grammarly, read it aloud, and edit appropriately. A sloppy email communicates that you are fulfilling an obligation rather than cultivating a relationship (Indeed Editorial Staff, 2024).

Building relationships over time doesn't end with your follow-up note or a single coffee meeting. This process requires a delicate balance of keeping in touch without overwhelming your contact. Consider setting reminders to check in periodically, perhaps every few months, with a brief update or a question. These touchpoints could be as simple as sharing an article related to their industry or congratulating them on a recent achievement. Even a LinkedIn message works.

Be sure to ask about them. If your introverted makeup includes a large dose of empathy, this goes without saying. If not, remember it's not all about you. If your contact previously mentioned being a project lead, ask how the project is progressing. If their recent initiatives have positively impacted your work, tell them so. You may need to do your homework to see what's happening in their world. But your word of encouragement might brighten their whole day and propel your relationship forward (Wojnicki, 2023).

Each interaction should feel natural and unforced, demonstrating your genuine interest in maintaining the connection. This practice solidifies your networking efforts and positions you as a thoughtful and engaged industry professional. Consistency is key. Relationships are built on trust. Regular, thoughtful communication reinforces this foundation.

Action Plan: Follow-Up Message

- **Improving:** Pull up a past networking follow-up email. Read it aloud and make 1–2 edits. Run it by your communications ally to get a second opinion. If it needs no improvement, good for you!
- **Prep:** Choose a specific upcoming network event and pinpoint three potential new

contacts. Write out 2–3 potential services you could offer each person. Write out three things you would appreciate learning or ways to collaborate with each contact.

11

CONTINUING TO BUILD YOUR COMMUNICATIONS REPERTOIRE

I prepared for moments like these as best I could. I spent the last year practicing public speaking every chance I could get. And I call this my "year of speaking dangerously."

— SUSAN CAIN SPEAKING OF HER TED TALK *THE POWER OF INTROVERTS*

Resilience in communication is the unshakeable grit that motivates you to remain composed even when conversations go awry. Each interaction, whether a casual chat at the coffee machine or a high-stakes negotiation, presents an opportunity to cultivate resilience, like developing a muscle over time. It is not merely about bouncing back from a misjudged comment or an awkward pause. It empowers you to confront and embrace discomfort when you falter in your presentation. Resilience encourages you to view mistakes as detours that offer new perspectives. Much like a sailboat adjusting its sails to navigate turbulent waters, your resilience allows you to adapt and thrive in diverse communicative landscapes. You persist, anticipate challenges, respond with agility, and learn from each experience to enhance future interactions.

Consider Emma, a project manager known for her meticulous attention to detail. During a pivotal presentation to senior executives, her PowerPoint stopped working. Rather than succumbing to the pressure and frustration, Emma acknowledged the issue with humor, engaged the audience with spontaneous anecdotes, and seamlessly transitioned back to her key points once the technical glitches were resolved. Her ability to recover not only salvaged the presentation but also demonstrated her capacity to handle unforeseen challenges. Emma's experience underscores the transformative power of resilience in navigating communication obstacles.

If resilience is so important, how do you build it? The top two activities needed to grow your communications resilience have been mentioned numerous times already in this book: active listening and practice. If you are serious about becoming a more resilient communicator, advance to role-playing more challenging conversations with your communications ally or trusted coworker (i.e., a conversation about downsizing or reallocating resources). Take public speaking opportunities. Per Toastmasters, engaging in regular public speaking builds your confidence and adaptability. "The more you expose yourself to different speaking scenarios, the more resilient you become in handling questions, interruptions, and nerves." You don't need to present to 100 people. Rather, choose something low-key. Offer to do a presentation to your team or another department at work (Olsen, 2024).

Building your emotional regulation skills will increase your resilience, too. You need to learn to tolerate distress and interruptions. This book isn't about anger management or controlling spontaneous urges. However, controlling your emotional expression is key to handling more complex communication situations. Working through feedback loops helps. Expanding on Chapter 8 when we discussed handling rejection, learn to thank the person giving you feedback and ask for examples and suggestions on how to improve. Doing this shows your commitment to self-growth and becoming a more resilient communicator (Olsen, 2024).

We live in a real world. Resilience is also about persisting through communication difficulties. Not every conversation will unfold flawlessly. It is not about achieving perfection but about embracing the process of growth.

Action Plan: Self-Assessment and Practice Building Resilience

- **Self-assessment:** Identify three recent communication challenges. Reflect on what caused each challenge: Was it a lack of preparation, miscommunication, or perhaps an emotional response? Divide a paper into two columns. On one side, write out the cause(s) for the communication mishap. Across from each cause, write out the actionable steps you will take to overcome it.
- **Presentation:** Do a presentation in a low-key environment. Practice aloud 2–3 times. Record and critique yourself. Ask for feedback from your communications ally or someone you trust who attended your presentation.

COMMUNICATING ACROSS CULTURES

Harvard Business School published Culturewizard's 2018 Virtual Teams Survey. It stated that 89% of corporate employees serve on at least one global team, and 62% have colleagues from three or more cultures (Gavin, 2019). In today's interconnected world, effective cross-cultural communication is the backbone of global business success.

It begins with cultural intelligence (CQ), the ability to relate to and work effectively across cultures. CQ is "an outsider's seemingly natural ability to interpret someone's unfamiliar and ambiguous gestures the way that person's compatriots would." It includes three components: cognitive, physical, and motivational. The words and actions of a person with CQ align to prove that they are entering into another culture's world (Earley & Mosakowski, 2004).

Thankfully, we can learn CQ and attain an acceptable level. Take Maria, who is welcoming a new international colleague from Japan. Before her colleague arrives, Maria takes the time to learn a few phrases in Japanese and studies Japanese social cues. Understanding Japanese cultural nuances, she opts for a warm yet respectful greeting, carefully avoiding direct eye contact, which can be seen as confrontational. By acknowledging her colleague's cultural background, Maria not only earns respect but also sets the stage for a productive working relationship.

Communication styles vary significantly worldwide because each culture influences them. However, understanding the differences between high-context and low-context communication raises your CQ significantly. High-context cultures rely heavily on implicit communication, where much is left unsaid. People in high-context cultures read between the lines, pay close attention to nonverbals, and interpret communication in view of the social roles of those involved. Good communication in high-context cultures is indirect and nuanced. Speakers often address a topic indirectly and look at it from divergent viewpoints. To capture meanings fully, they focus less on words and more on contextual elements like tone of voice, social status, body language, and physical settings. India, China, Saudi Arabia, Japan, most African countries, and South Korea are the dominant highest-context cultures globally.

In contrast, low-context cultures pay more attention to words in communication rather than nonverbals or the speaker's social position. Speakers want their messages to be accurate, simple, clear, and interpreted literally. They value repetition, summaries, and setting clear expectations. They want their communication to be explicit, leaving little room for ambiguity. The information on effective communication in Chapter 3 makes it obvious that I am writing from a low-context communication style. Specifically, I am an American. Australia, Canada, the Netherlands, and Germany also follow low-context communication styles (Pascual, 2022).

When speakers of high-context and low-context styles communicate with each other, misunderstanding and confusion occur until both parties address their differences and agree on a common communication style for the workplace. The following dialogue taken from The Culture Map by Erin Meyer (Meyer, 2016) illustrates the problem. Mr. Díaz, a Spanish executive, is talking to his Chinese employee, Mr. Chen, about working on Sunday. Here's their conversation:

> Mr. Díaz: It looks like some of us are going to have to be here on Sunday to host the client visit.

> Mr. Chen: I see.

> Mr. Díaz: Can you join us on Sunday?

> Mr. Chen: Yes, I think so.

> Mr. Díaz: That would be a great help.

> Mr. Chen: Yes, Sunday is an important day.

> Mr. Díaz: In what way?

> Mr. Chen: It's my daughter's birthday.

> Mr. Díaz: How nice. I hope you all enjoy it.

> Mr. Chen: Thank you. I appreciate your understanding.

Both men believe they are being very clear. Yet they are both missing each other's hints. Mr. Diaz comes from a low-context with a more direct communication style. Mr. Chen is from a high-context culture. Mr. Díaz is expecting to see Mr. Chen on Sunday, while Chen is sure his boss has accepted his excuse. After all, what father (Chen's social position) would miss his child's birthday? It's noteworthy that Chen doesn't come right out and say, "I'm not coming on Sunday."

Since I operate within a low-context style, here are some suggestions for communicating with speakers from high-context cultures. It's better to stay away from yes/no questions as they are too direct and make people from high-context cultures uncomfortable. Instead, gravitate to open-ended questions. This allows you to elicit some of the implied context from your high-context culture colleague. Think about your colleague's social position (i.e., parent, elderly, rich) Pay attention when you hear the phrases "I will think about it," "I guess so," "I will do my best," and "It will be very difficult, but I am going to give it a try." Your coworker likely feels cornered. Switch to open-ended questions to dig deeper (Pascual, 2022).

Not speaking the same language is an obvious cause of cross-cultural communication blunders, especially when one party is learning a second language (i.e., a Canadian engineer learning Mandarin). Here are a few other key cultural communication differences to ponder when interacting at work:

- **Conflict resolution styles:** Some cultures prefer open confrontation to resolve conflict, while others prioritize harmony and avoid direct disagreement.
- **Power distance:** Cultures with high power distance expect deference to authority figures, while those with low power distance encourage more open discussion and debate. This principle has huge implications in terms of giving and receiving feedback. (*High vs. Low Power Distance Culture,* n.d.)
- **Decision-making process:** Some cultures prioritize consensus building (collectivism), while others may rely on individual leadership to make decisions (individualism).
- **Formality:** Different cultures have varying levels of formality in how they address colleagues. In hierarchical cultures or even the

military, speakers recognize a person's age, accomplishment, and educational status when they address the other person.

Understanding these cultural aspects can guide you in promoting collaboration, providing feedback, and addressing conflicts delicately, ensuring that interactions remain respectful and constructive. If you have a new international coworker or will be traveling internationally, research cultural norms and practices before your interactions begin. Pay particular attention to gestures and body language. What might be considered a friendly gesture in one culture could be perceived as offensive in another. For instance, a thumbs-up is a positive sign in the West but can be considered rude in parts of the Middle East. Familiarizing yourself with these nuances can prevent inadvertent offenses and create a more respectful dialogue.

Asking open-ended questions is another powerful technique to clarify cultural nuances and promote mutual understanding. Instead of making assumptions, invite your international colleagues to share their perspectives. Questions like, "How do you prefer to receive feedback?" or "What is the best way to address concerns in your work culture?" can provide valuable insights into their preferences and expectations. By engaging in open dialogue, you demonstrate respect for their cultural background and make them feel welcome, valued, and heard.

Action Plan: Cultural Exploration Exercise

- **Cultural research:** Choose the culture of an international colleague. Define it in terms of high-context vs. low-context, individualistic vs collective, and high power distance vs. low power distance. Bonus points for researching if it is a shame-based culture. (Look it up. That's part of the extra credit.)
- **Communication research:** For the same culture, research appropriate and inappropriate gestures, forms of politeness and formal address, relevant cultural norms/values, and their views of your home culture (i.e., What do they like or dislike about the British?).
- **Specific questions:** Write down three questions you can ask your colleague about their home culture's work environment and expectations. For example, "How do you prefer I communicate about," "How would you like to be addressed?" or "How did you give suggestions in meetings there? Ask your coworker your questions. Your sincere attempts to bridge your cultures will earn you respect.

12

MORE INTERACTIVE EXERCISES AND SELF-ASSESSMENT

Communication works for those who work at it.

— JOHN POWELL (FILM COMPOSER)

Buying this book and making it through to Chapter 12 already indicates that you are serious about improving your business communication skills. You likely see it as a necessity for personal growth and to climb the career ladder. But the question on the table now is: What comes next in your communications growth journey?

The only way to continue growing your communication skills is to make them a priority. Communication is not a static skill but a dynamic one that evolves with practice and reflection. It's a skill that can be honed over time, much like a craftsperson refining their art. You need to commit time and effort daily to improving your skill set. If you don't, it will fall to the bottom of your priority list, which is never good (Hensley, 2024).

A great first step is to seek out great role models. Learn from the best communicators Look for a "natural," knowing that person probably worked very hard on their own skill set. Who is available to you? Is there someone at work who's a masterful storyteller? Who gives the best presentations? Once you select one or two people, watch them closely to analyze what makes them so skilled. What are they doing right? Consider their use of body language, pacing (including strategic pauses), word choices, and ability to read the room. You can emulate some of their moves without giving up who you are (i.e., pausing in the same places in your presentations, asking the same types of small talk questions). Ask them for specific pointers (Roberts, 2023).

Another step is to discover your unique communication style, your strengths, and the areas ripe for growth. We all possess the subtle nuances of our communication patterns. Knowing your own style and that of your coworkers empowers you to communicate more effectively. You can find your style using a free online communication style quiz that only takes a few minutes to complete. These quizzes are akin to a mirror, reflecting your natural tendencies and highlighting areas for improvement. By answering questions about your interactions and preferences, these inventories identify and categorize your style. Are you an analytical communicator who values data and logic, or perhaps a more intuitive one, guided by emotions and connections?

Leadership IQ and Verywellmind both offer free quizzes but test for very different components. The free assessment from VeryWellMind divides its categories based on passive, aggressive, passive-aggressive, and assertive (Nelson & Ingalls, 2023). Leadership IQ classifies styles based on analytical, intuitive, functional, and personal. (Murphy, 2017). Their testing criteria are complementary. Both companies give good explanations of their categories, citing both strengths and areas for improvement. However, Leadership IQ includes a component that addresses different communication styles on teams.

Continuing regular communication self-assessments is a wise move, too. By continuing to record yourself during presentations or meetings, you can review your verbal and nonverbal communication to refine your delivery. Adding an outsider's perspective with online video-based assessments will propel your growth even further. Video-based assessments offer the advantage of receiving feedback, either from peers or through AI-enhanced tools, which can highlight areas for growth that you might overlook. Platforms like GoReact (2024) offer innovative ways to assess and develop your communication competence.

Action Plan

- **Role model:** Choose a communications role model from work. If you can't find a suitable candidate at work, think of a speaker you enjoy listening to outside of work. Consider TED talk speakers, professors, or religious teachers rather than TV personalities or political figures.
- **Communication style quiz:** Take at least one online communications style test.
- **Evaluation:** Schedule monthly self-evaluation checkups using your recordings. You can also subscribe to an online service like GoReact to evaluate your communication regularly.

SUSTAINING LONG-TERM COMMUNICATION GROWTH

Marathon runners don't just prepare for a race. Most train for a lifetime of fitness and endurance. Much like training for distance running, your communication skills require ongoing attention and refinement. Setting long-term communication goals is akin to planning your training regimen. It's a guide that positions you to hone your abilities as you evolve professionally. Establishing realistic and meaningful goals helps you stay focused and have a growth mindset. The beauty of long-term goals lies in their ability to transform aspirations into achievements.

The first step is creating a communication development plan. This plan serves as your blueprint, outlining the steps you will take to enhance your skills systematically. Your plan will be a living document that adapts to your evolving needs and priorities. To illustrate, let's consider two examples of communication development plans. In the first scenario, you might focus on enhancing your public speaking skills. Your plan could include attending monthly workshops, practicing speeches in front of a mirror, and seeking peer feedback for small presentations. In the second example, you might aim to improve your cross-cultural communication skills. Your plan could involve enrolling in a cultural sensitivity course, engaging in language exchange programs, and participating in international networking events.

Once your communication development plan is in place, set milestones and review your progress regularly. Aligning your milestones with project completions or mastering skills are good options. For example, evaluate after your team has launched a new product or service. Or, check your growth after you've increased your second language vocabulary or successfully navigated board meetings. At each milestone, assess your progress, target new areas for improvement, and adjust your pace if needed. Quarterly evaluation tools work well for tracking your progress. Revamping your development plan each year will help you remain accountable for your goals and motivated to continue your journey.

Incorporate retaking communication style assessments into your plan to see if your styles have changed. When my new job responsibilities became public speaking and interaction-driven, I moved from being very introverted to near the middle line between introvert/extrovert. Revisiting your communication assessments helps you stay attuned to your evolving preferences, strengths, and needs. If you change jobs or roles within your company or team, see how the shift might have impacted your style or how your style might need to shift because of new communication demands. Understanding these changes can help you tailor your communication approach to suit your current needs and goals.

Be a lifelong learner who is open to new experiences and perspectives. Seek diverse learning opportunities where you can explore new communication techniques and gain insights from experts in the field. Attending workshops and seminars is an excellent way to expand your knowledge and connect with like-minded individuals. Just be sure to intersperse some in-person events between the virtual ones. Face-to-face communication introduces more complex variables to navigate than webinars. Use some of your business account funds to pay for books, podcasts, and online courses.

Mastering storytelling is a great option. Even Forbes advocates it: "If you want to get better results communicating, make room for storytelling" (Alnaghmoosh, 2023). Stories are more memorable and engaging than other types of communication. They bring data to life and make complex topics more palatable. They contextualize information and make it relatable because they create mental pictures. If those weren't enough reasons to study storytelling, stories also create an emotional connection with your audience and build trust. This connection translated into more engagement with you, your company, and your brand.

Don't worry. Business storytelling won't remind you of your kid's bedtime ritual. It focuses on conveying a message rather than entertaining. Think of case studies, origin stories, ads, and impact stories. Work your way through storytelling books like Guy Kawasaki's *Selling the Dream* (Kawasaki, 1992) or Sanchez and Duarte's *Illuminate* (Duarte & Sanchez, 2016).

Remember that growth is a dynamic and ongoing process. It requires patience, perseverance, and a willingness to step outside your comfort zone. Embrace challenges as opportunities for learning, and view setbacks as stepping stones toward greater proficiency. By maintaining a growth mindset, you cultivate resilience and adaptability, empowering you to navigate the ever-changing landscape of professional communication.

Action Plan

- **Development plan:** Write out a development plan that includes two aspects of your communication you would like to improve. Include 2 to 4 concrete actions you will take to make growth a reality. Set your evaluation date with an alarm on your calendar.
- **Take action:** Choose two skill-building

resources you would like to attend or buy. Then, follow through with your purchase.

CONCLUSION

I think introverts can do quite well,... If you're clever, you can learn to get the benefits of being an introvert.

— BILL GATES

Bill Gates's quote nails it: You can do quite well while still being authentically you. As you leverage your introverted superpowers, like active listening and empathy, you're moving closer to realizing your full potential to be an effective and impactful communicator. You're becoming more attuned to your strengths and communication style, picking up on subtle communication nuances more and more. You know where you are headed, and you have a communications development plan to get you there. You are on your way.

Congratulations on your progress! You and your communication ally or trusted coworker have been working hard to transform you into a stellar communicator at work. They deserve a steak dinner, so treat them as a thank you. If they're vegan, my daughter would recommend spicy Thai stir fry with tofu. You both deserve to celebrate!

But, before you go, let's recap our time together with a good low-context communication style summary. Being an effective communicator at work doesn't mean that you need to mimic extroverts' communication strategies. Absolutely not! As an introvert, you can shine as a business world communicator with your deep listening, empathy, thoughtful reflection, and innovative problem-solving. Your innate ability to focus and analyze can be a significant advantage.

In each communication situation you encounter, you can build rapport with your coworkers, superiors, or clients as you listen more than you speak. You've learned the importance of asking open-ended questions and being culturally sensitive. By doing your homework and practicing consistent verbal and nonverbal communication, you can upgrade your daily conversations or your weekly team meeting contributions. Using your breathing techniques and reciting your mantras, you can engage more confidently in spontaneous conversations, negotiations, and even upward communication. Even networking events won't be quite as hard on you because you're setting realistic goals and have a great elevator pitch ready to share at the opportune moment.

Not every sentence you say will be flawless, and that's okay. Sometimes, your timing may be off, or a microexpression might leak out. But you recognize each conversation as an opportunity to practice and refine the skills you've acquired. You will persist, repeating your presentations in front of the bathroom mirror, listening for clumsy filler words, and checking your tone of voice in your recordings. You might even sign up for Toastmasters or German cultural studies to keep expanding your communications repertoire.

When you need inspiration going forward, think of Ben Silbermann, the co-founder and CEO of Pinterest, who has left his indelible mark on the world of social media and visual discovery. Or remember Satoshi Tajiri, the creative genius behind Pokémon. Let immigrant Nina Vaca blow you away with her rags-to-riches story. At age 25, with just $300, she founded the workforce solutions firm, the Pinnacle Group. Pinnacle is now a billion-dollar enterprise in 10 countries and one of the fastest-growing U.S. women-owned businesses. Vaca embraced the strengths she brought to the table, honed her expertise, and built a reputation around her natural abilities. Each of these introverts achieved remarkable business success by being themselves (Pollard, 2023).

You may never become famous. But when you embrace and nurture your introverted strengths in communication, you can achieve professional and personal success. You can connect deeply with your audiences and build rapport into long-standing business relationships. Keep practicing, fellow introvert!

Thank you for allowing me to guide you through this journey. Here's to your continued success and growth in both your career and personal life. The world needs your voice. Go out there and be heard!

REFERENCES

5 Breathing Exercises to Tackle Anxiety from your Desk | Action Mental Health. (2023, May 12). Action Mental Health | Enhancing Quality of Life and Employability for People with Mental Health Needs.; Action Mental Health. https://www.amh.org.uk/5-breathing-exercises-to-tackle-anxiety-from-your-desk/

7 Universal Facial Expressions. What Do They Mean? | Betterhelp. (n.d.). Www.betterhelp.com. https://www.betterhelp.com/advice/body-language/7-universal-facial-expressions-what-do-they-mean/

12 Tips to Have Better Conversations in the Workplace. (2024). Coffeepals.com. https://www.coffeepals.com/blog/12-tips-to-have-better-conversations-in-the-workplace

30 of literature's most inspirational quotes about strength. (2019). Stylist.co.uk. https://www.stylist.co.uk/books/quotes/quotes-about-strength-from-literature/299768

101 Quotes to inspire speakers. (2016, December 23). SpeakerHub. https://speakerhub.com/blog/101-quotes

Alnaghmoosh, A. (2023, June 21). *Storytelling: Inspiring Audiences In Business Development.* Forbes https://www.forbes.com/councils/forbesbusinessdevelopmentcouncil/2023/06/21/the-power-of-storytelling-inspiring-audiences-in-business-development/#:~:text=What%20makes%20storytelling%20such%20an,your%20audience%20and%20create%20relatability.

Autenrieth, N. (2018, May 10). *Networking for Introverts: The Ultimate Guide.* TopResume; Networking for Introverts: The Ultimate Guide | TopResume. https://topresume.com/career-advice/networking-tips-for-introverts

Back Intelligence. (2019). 5 Stretches At Your Desk (Without Getting Up) [YouTube Video]. In *YouTube*. https://www.youtube.com/watch?v=nFIfv-jIgbI

Balancing Your Time and Energy as an Introvert. (2018). Psychology Today. https://www.psychologytoday.com/us/blog/self-promotion-for-introverts/201803/balancing-your-time-and-energy-as-an-introvert

BBC Bitesize. (2019, October 13). *The introverts' guide to negotiation: 14 steps to success! - BBC Bitesize.* BBC Bitesize. https://www.bbc.co.uk/bitesize/articles/zhqcvk7

Be Better at Spontaneous Speaking. (n.d.). Stanford Graduate School of Business. https://www.gsb.stanford.edu/insights/be-better-spontaneous-speaking

Besieux, T., Edmondson, A. C., & Vries, F. de. (2021, June 11). *How to Overcome Your Fear of Speaking Up in Meetings.* Harvard Business Review. https://hbr.org/2021/06/how-to-overcome-your-fear-of-speaking-up-in-meetings

Bloch, R. (2015, October 10). *"What You Do Speaks So Loudly I Cannot Hear What You Are Saying."* Medium. https://medium.com/golden-eggs/what-you-do-speaks-so-loudly-i-cannot-hear-what-you-are-saying-92fbfdf52472

Brooks, A. W. (2013). Get Excited: Reappraising Pre-Performance Anxiety as Excitement. *Journal of Experimental Psychology.* https://www.hbs.edu/ris/Publication%20Files/xge-a0035325%20(2)_0287835d-9e25-4f92-9661-c5b54dbbcb39.pdf

Brown, Brené. (2021). *Atlas of the heart: mapping meaningful connection and the language of human experience.* Random House.

Brown, Brené. (2018). *Brené Brown*. Brené Brown. https://brenebrown.com/

Brown, Brené. (2010). *The gifts of imperfection: let go of who you think you're supposed to be and embrace who you are*. Hazelden.

Burton, T. (2023, November 8). *10 Tips for Active Listening*. PBI; Pennsylvania Bar Institute. https://go.pbi.org/blog/10-tips-for-active-listening#:~:text=Do%20not%20let%20your%20emotions,Improvement%20will%20come%20over%20time.

Cain, S. (2013). *Quiet: The power of introverts in a world that can't stop talking*. Broadway Books.

Castrillon, C. (2019). How Introverts can thrive as entrepreneurs [Review of *How Introverts can thrive as entrepreneurs*]. *Forbes*.

Cerebral Blood Flow and Personality: A Positron Emission Tomography Study (1999, February 1). Psychiatry Online; The American Journal of Psychiatry. https://psychiatryonline.org/doi/full/10.1176/ajp.156.2.252

Chazin, S. (2024, September 18). *Quiet Zones and Power Hours: Maximizing Your Productivity as an Introvert*. Medium. https://medium.com/@stacey_76464/quiet-zones-and-power-hours-maximizing-your-productivity-as-an-introvert-6c962452718d

Coles, J. (2023, April 3). *7 Actions To Practice Diplomacy at Work*. Enhance Training. https://enhance.training/7-actions-to-practice-diplomacy-at-work-avoid-offending-colleagues-tm0169/

Contributor, J. B. (2021, August 17). *People who are good at small talk always avoid these 7 mistakes, says public speaking expert*. CNBC. https://www.cnbc.com/2021/08/17/avoid-these-mistakes-if-you-want-to-be-good-at-small-talk-says-public-speaking-expert.html

Cuncic, A. (2024, February 12). *7 Active Listening Techniques For Better Communication*. Verywell Mind. https://www.verywellmind.com/what-is-active-listening-3024343#:~:text=2.,any%20type%20of%20negative%20response. Medically reviewed by Amy Morin, LCSW.

Dare To Be Active with Dr. LA Thoma Gustin. (2019). DAILY DESK STRETCHES - Stretches to do at your desk to prevent pain | Dr. LA Thoma Gustin [YouTube Video]. In *YouTube*. https://www.youtube.com/watch?v=vBQkySm333k

de Paul, L. (2024, September 10). *The Power of Introverts: Lessons from Successful Business Owners*. Forbes.

Duarte, N., & Sanchez, P. (2016). *Illuminate: ignite change through speeches, stories, ceremonies, and symbols*. Duarte Press.

Earley, P. C., & Mosakowski, E. (2004, October). *Cultural Intelligence.* Harvard Business Review. https://hbr.org/2004/10/cultural-intelligence

Edwards, V. V. (2019, March 6). *20 Hand Gestures You Should Be Using.* Medium. https://medium.com/@vvanedwards/20-hand-gestures-you-should-be-using-c8717eca02d7

Excel in Spontaneous Conversations. (2024, February 15). All the Hacks with Chris Hutchins. https://www.chrishutchins.com/blog/excel-in-spontaneous-conversations/

Gavin, M. (2019, May 16). *6 Tips for Managing Global & International Teams.* Harvard Business School Online. https://online.hbs.edu/blog/post/how-to-manage-global-teams)

Gaunt, D. (2021). Understanding Negotiation Roles and Responsibilities. *Blackswanltd.com.* https://doi.org/10872003531/module_156190566779_mega-menu-lang-switcher

GoReact. (2024, August 13). *How to Assess Communication Skills | Top Insights & Methods.* Video Assessment for Skill Development & Feedback | GoReact. https://get.goreact.com/resources/how-to-assess-communication-skills/

Green, H. (2018, September 18). *Active Listening As A Leadership Skill | Vistage*. Vistage Research Center. https://www.vistage.com/research-center/business-leadership/20180912-active-listening-leadership-skill/

Gupta, P. (2023, November 3). *6 Simple Steps to Enhance Speech Clarity and Connect with Confidence*. 1SpecialPlace. https://www.1specialplace.com/post/6-simple-steps-to-enhance-speech-clarity

Helgoe, L. A. (2013). *Introvert Power*. Sourcebooks, Inc.

Hensley, M. (2024, June 4). *7 Tips to Improve Your Business Communication Skills*. Startup Nation. https://startupnation.com/

High vs. Low Power Distance Culture | Definition & Examples. Study.Com. https://study.com/academy/lesson/comparing-low-high-power-distance-cultural-communications.html#:~:text=Power%20distance%20is%20the%20range,distributed%20more%20equally%20among%20members.

Holt, T. (2024, October 8). *The Power of Authentic Communication: Building Trust and Connection in Business*. Wood Industry. https://woodindustry.ca/the-power-of-authentic-communication-building-trust-and-connection-in-business/#:~:text=In%20business%20communication%2C%20authenticity%20means,how%20your%20message%20is%20received.

How to Cope With Social Anxiety When You Have a Meeting at Work. (2019). Verywell Mind. https://www.verywell mind.com/anxiety-in-meetings-3024310

How to handle rejection gracefully: 10 mindful tips for moving on — Calm Blog. (n.d.). *Calm Blog.* https://www.calm.com/blog/how-to-handle-rejection

Indeed Editorial Staff. (2024, August 15). *How To Write a Networking Follow-Up Email (Plus 5 Samples).* Indeed. https://www.indeed.com/career-advice/career-development/networking-follow-up-email

Inspiring Marissa Mayer Quotes To Get You Through The Work Day. (2017). Fairygodboss. https://fairygodboss.com/career-topics/marissa-mayer-quotes

International, F. (2024). *Can rejection make you resilient?* Fiu.edu. https://business.fiu.edu/academics/graduate/insights/posts/can-rejection-make-you-resilient.html

Janssen, A. (2021, September 29). *7 Ways to Set Availability Boundaries and Reduce Interruptions.* Ashley Janssen Consulting. https://ashleyjanssen.com/7-ways-to-set-availability-boundaries-and-reduce-interruptions/

Jess. (2024, June 19). *Building Trust through Nonverbal Cues: A Guide for Business Professionals.* Inspirepreneur. https://inspirepreneurmagazine.com/building-trust-through-nonverbal-cues-a-guide-for-business-professionals/

Jones, L. (2020, September 10). Global consulting firm finds success with "introvert hour." *Harvard Business Review*. https://hbr.org/2020/09/global-consulting-firm-finds-success-with-introvert-hour

Jones, M. (2020, February 27). *10 Common Hand Gestures That Are Rude in Other Countries*. Reader's Digest. https://www.rd.com/article/common-hand-gestures-rude-in-other-countries/

Kane, E. (2023, February 12). *Review of Introvert Book #3: The Introvert Advantage by Martin Olsen Laney, Psy.D.* Esther Kane. https://www.estherkane.com/review-of-introvert-book-3-the-introvert-advantage-by-martin-olsen-laney-psy-d/#:~:text=Introverted%20people%20who%20balance%20their,stimulating%20environment%20provides%20for%20introverts.

Kawasaki, G. (1992). *Selling the dream: how to promote your product, company, or ideas - and make a difference - using everyday evangelism*. Harperbusiness.

King, P. (2020). *Better Small Talk*. PKCS Media.

Laney, M. O. (2013). *The Introvert Advantage: How to Thrive in an Extrovert World*. HighBridge Company.

Latz, M. (2024, December). *The Five Golden Rules of Negotiation for lawyers*. Oregon State Bar. https://www.osbar.org/publications/bulletin/04dec/tips.html#:~:text=1.,an%20agreement%20is%20not%20reached

Lynette. (2018, March 26). *It Is Possible For Introverts To Be Persuasive - Quiet Brilliance Consulting*. Quiet Brilliance Consulting. https://quietbrillianceconsulting.com/it-is-possible-for-introverts-to-be-persuasive/

Marolewski, P. (n.d.). *How to use Mantras for Professional Success*. Forbes.

Media, T. (2022, November 29). *How to Succeed in Business Negotiations (Even If You Are an Introvert!)*. ThriveDX. https://thrivedx.com/resources/blog/how-to-succeed-in-business-negotiations-even-if-you-are-an-introvert

Meyer, E. (2016). *The Culture Map: Breaking Through the Invisible Boundaries of Global Business* (1st ed.). Publicaffairs.

Morin, A., 2020, #91 Why It Benefits You to Become a Better Listener [Audio podcast episode]. The Verywell Mind Podcast, Verywell Mind, https://megaphone.link/MERE4156868721

Murphy, M. (2017). *Quiz: What's Your Communication Style?* Leadership IQ. https://www.leadershipiq.com/

blogs/leadershipiq/39841409-quiz-whats-your-communication-style

Naysmith, C. (n.d.). *Warren Buffett's Essential Golden Rule: "Go Into Business Only With People Whom You Like, Trust, and Admire."* MSN. https://www.msn.com/en-us/money/savingandinvesting/warren-buffett-s-essential-golden-rule-go-into-business-only-with-people-whom-you-like-trust-and-admire/ar-AA1wFwpw

Nelson, K., & Ingalls, N. (2023, October 17). *What's Your Communication Style? Take the Quiz and Find Out.* Very Well Mind. https://www.verywellmind.com/take-the-communication-style-quiz-7973143

The Neuroscience Behind Introversion and What It Means For You In Conflict – Novel HR. (n.d.).https://novelhr.ca/the-neuroscience-behind-introversion-and-what-it-means-for-you-in-conflict/

O'Connor, C. (2012). How Sara Blakely of Spanx Turned $5,000 into $1 billion [Review of *How Sara Blakely of Spanx Turned $5,000 into $1 billion*]. Forbes.

Olsen, R. (2024, October 22). *Building Resilience in Communication.* Toastmasters International. https://www.d16toastmasters.org/building-resilience-in-communication/#:~:text=Tips%20for%20Building%20Resilient%20Communication%20Skills&text=Give%

20the%20speaker%20your%20full,respect%20and%20helps%20build%20trust

Overcoming a meeting slump: how to stay focused during board meetings. (2020, June 7). IBabs. https://www.ibabs.com/en/general/overcoming-a-meeting-slump-how-to-stay-focused-during-board-meetings/

Overvest, M. (n.d.). *13 Best Negotiators 2025 — Famous Experts* [Review of *13 Best Negotiators 2025 — Famous Experts*]. Procurement Tactics. https://procurementtactics.com/best-negotiator/

Pascual, P. (2022, October 11). *High-Context Cultures – Avoid Misunderstandings And Build Stronger Relationships.* Talaera. https://www.talaera.com/blog/high-context-cultures-avoid-misunderstandings-and-build-stronger-relationships/

Pollack, J., & Pollack, J. (2024, September 4). *Body Language in the Workplace: Tips & Why It's so Powerful - Defuse - De-Escalation Training.* Defuse - De-Escalation Training. https://deescalation-training.com/2024/09/body-language-in-the-workplace/

Pollard, M. (2023, January 2). *How Introverts Can Become Successful Entrepreneurs: 10 Inspiring Stories.* The Introverts Edge; Matthewpollard.com. https://matthewpollard.com/theintrovertsedge/successful-introvert-entrepreneurs

Psychology Today Staff. (n.d.). *Persuasion*. Psychology Today. https://www.psychologytoday.com/us/basics/persuasion

The Quiet Power of Saying No: The Introvert's Guide to Setting Boundaries | LifeAt. (2025). Lifeat.io. https://lifeat.io/blog/crisp-air-clear-mind-the-introverts-guide-to-setting-boundaries

A quote by Warren Buffett. (2024). Goodreads.com. https://www.goodreads.com/quotes/801715-you-ve-gotta-keep-control-of-your-time-and-you-can-t

Ramki, H. (2024, November 26). *11 actually great elevator pitch examples and how to make yours*. Zapier. https://zapier.com/blog/elevator-pitch-example/

Rauch, J. (2003, March 1). *Caring for Your Introvert*. The Atlantic. https://www.theatlantic.com/magazine/archive/2003/03/caring-for-your-introvert/302696/

Reframing negative thoughts: how to challenge negative thinking. (n.d.).Calm. https://www.calm.com/blog/reframing-negative-thoughts?undefined&utm_medium=organic&utm_source=blog&utm_campaign=how-to-handle-rejection

Clinically reviewed by Dr. Chris Mosunic.

Reynolds, G. (2019, May 14). How one tech company created spaces for introverts to thrive. New York

Times. https://www.nytimes.com/2019/05/14/business/introverts-in-the-workplace.html

Roberts, E. (2023, December 5). *19 communications tips for building your confidence at work*. Agility PR Solutions. https://www.agilitypr.com/pr-news/public-relations/19-communications-tips-for-building-your-confidence-at-work/

The Role Body Language Plays in Professional Settings | Walden University. (n.d.). Www.waldenu.edu. https://www.waldenu.edu/programs/business/resource/the-role-body-language-plays-in-professional-settings

Sen, J. (2024, April 8). *What is Empathic Communication and Why is Empathy Important?* Prezentium. https://prezentium.com/what-is-empathic-communication/

Schultz, J. (2012, December 13). *Eye contact: Don't make these mistakes*. Michigan State University; MSU Extension. https://www.canr.msu.edu/news/eye_contact_dont_make_these_mistakes

Schwantes, M. (2021, November 8). *In a Few Words, Warren Buffett Reminds Us of a Forgotten Habit That Led to His Success*. Inc. https://www.inc.com/marcel-schwantes/in-a-few-words-warren-buffett-reminds-us-of-a-forgotten-habit-that-led-to-his-success.html

Sen, J. (2024, April 8). *What is Empathic Communication and Why is it Important at the Workplace?* Prezentium. https://prezentium.com/what-is-empathic-communication/

Shen, X., Wu, Q., & Fu, X. (2012). Effects of the duration of expressions on the recognition of microexpressions. *Journal of Zhejiang University SCIENCE B, 13*(3), 221–230. https://doi.org/10.1631/jzus.b1100063

Sizemore, C. (2013, May 8). The Worst Investment Of Warren Buffett's Career. *Forbes.* https://www.forbes.com/sites/moneybuilder/2013/05/08/the-worst-investment-of-warren-buffetts-career/

The Speaker Lab. (2024, June 10). *How to Use Hand Gestures to Improve Communication.* The Speaker Lab. https://thespeakerlab.com/blog/hand-gestures/

Staff, P. (2024, October 1). *Negotiation Skills for Win-Win Negotiations.* Program on Negotiation; Harvard Law School. https://www.pon.harvard.edu/daily/negotiation-skills-daily/listening-skills-for-maximum-success/

Staff, P. (2024, October 29). *Negotiating Skills: Learn How to Build Trust at the Negotiation Table.* Program on Negotiation; Harvard Law School. https://www.pon.harvard.edu/daily/dealmaking-daily/dealmaking-negotiations-how-to-build-trust-at-the-bargaining-table/

Stevens, S. M. (2017). *Create your best work: How to maximize performance, minimize stress, and lead a balanced life.* Wiley.

Stinnett, J. (2018, February 12). *How to Persuade as an Analytical Introvert.* Jason Stinnett. https://jasonstinnett.com/blog/persuade-as-analytical-introvert

Team Duarte. (2024, September 27). *10 reasons why it's important to communicate with empathy and authority in times of crisis.* Duarte. https://www.duarte.com/blog/important-communicate-empathy-authority-times-crisis/

Tidwell, C. (2016). *Non Verbal Communication.* Andrews.edu. https://www.andrews.edu/~tidwell/bsad560/NonVerbal.html

Tips for Communicating Effectively With Your Boss. (n.d.). Www.eannc.com. https://www.eannc.com/employees/tips-for-communicating-effectively-with-your-boss

Tips to Stop Shyness from Holding You Back at Work. (n.d.). HiCounselor. https://icounselor.com/blog/career-insight/tips-to-stop-shyness-from-holding-you-back-at-work)

Using Empathy in Communication. (n.d.).Physiopedia. https://www.physio-pedia.com/Using_Empathy_in_

Communication#:~:text=Listen%20without%20interruption,amount%20of%20time%20has%20passed

Walters, H. (2014, October 31). *Vulnerability is the birthplace of innovation, creativity and change: Brené Brown at TED2012*. TED Blog; TED Blog. https://blog.ted.com/vulnerability-is-the-birthplace-of-innovation-creativity-and-change-brene-brown-at-ted2012/

Wayshak, M. (2015, February 18). *How Sales Legend Frank Perdue Overcame Shyness and Built a Business Empire*. Entrepreneur. https://www.entrepreneur.com/leadership/how-sales-legend-frank-perdue-overcame-shyness-and-built-a/242998

Wellness Wednesday: The golden 20 20 20 rule. (2020). Blood.ca. https://www.blood.ca/en/wellnesswednesday/golden%2020-20-20-rule

Westover, J. (2024). Harnessing the Power of Quiet: How Introverts Can Make a Big Impact in Organizations. *Human Capital Leadership Review*. https://www.innovativehumancapital.com/article/harnessing-the-power-of-quiet-how-introverts-can-make-a-big-impact-in-organizations

Why introverts are the best negotiators | Produced by Seattle Times Marketing. (2019, May 9). The Seattle Times. https://www.seattletimes.com/explore/careers/why-introverts-are-the-best-negotiators/

Winter, R. (2022, October 5). *Don't Be A Wallflower–How to Overcome Shyness at Work*. Harvard Resource Solutions. https://www.hrsus.com/2022/10/05/dont-be-a-wallflower-how-to-overcome-shyness-at-work/

Wojnicki, A. (2023, August 22). *Drop the Rehearsed Elevator Pitch and Try This Instead*. Inc. https://www.inc.com/andrea-wojnicki/drop-rehearsed-elevator-pitch-try-this-instead.html

Zimmer, J. (2009, December 7). *Mark Twain on public speaking nerves (everyone has them)*. Manner of Speaking. https://mannerofspeaking.org/2009/12/07/quotes-for-public-speakers-no-1/

www.ingramcontent.com/pod-product-compliance
Lightning Source LLC
Chambersburg PA
CBHW060947050426
42337CB00052B/1629